TEACHING FOR
CHANGE

Eight Keys
for Transformational
Bible Study with Teens

KEN COLEY

© 2017 by Ken Coley
Published by Randall House Publications
114 Bush Road
Nashville, TN 37217

Printed in the United States of America
13-ISBN 9780892659722

To my dad,

Richard Albert Coley

My favorite Bible teacher in my youth
and my lifelong example of living for Christ.

TABLE OF CONTENTS

INTRODUCTION

For her it was the most extraordinary encounter of her life. Like countless days before she was going about the most mundane of tasks, until Jesus engaged her in a conversation that led to her transformation. And it began with a simple request:

"Give Me a drink..."

Followed by powerful insights about God and Himself:

"If you knew the gift of God, and who is saying, 'Give Me a drink,' you would ask Him, and He would give you living water."

As the conversation developed, He continued to teach and connect the dots:

"Everyone who drinks from this water will get thirsty again..."

As the dialogue continued, she expressed partial understanding and awareness:

"I know that Messiah is coming..."

At that moment He concluded their conversation by revealing His identity:

"I am He, the One speaking to you."

Wow, we all would love to have insights into how Jesus taught so we could begin to see transformation in our group members' lives like the change demonstrated by the Samaritan woman that day. Unfortunately, many teachers mistakenly think that because they have attended many classes or Bible studies, they are ready to lead one.

A familiar story...

Nathan could not wait to get started. Since being recruited to lead a Bible study group, he had laid careful plans and worked tirelessly to prepare for this ministry—teaching his first Bible study session. With a few moments before class was scheduled to begin, Nathan took time to reflect on his preparations that included contacting each group member personally, organizing welcoming materials, and connecting with the group as a whole through social media. Lots of planning went into organizing the room, greeting visitors, and serving snacks. It was time to lead in prayer and start the lesson. And then it hit him...what was he supposed to do to teach the lesson? A sudden wave of fear swept over Nathan as he came to the realization that he didn't have a clue what to do for the next 45 minutes.

Working with the extraordinary team at Randall House has allowed me the opportunity to develop this book that summarizes my lifelong pursuit to collect keys to unlock the secrets to exceptional teaching. We decided to call this key ring of ideas, *Teaching for Change: Eight Keys for Transformational Bible Study with Teens*. I'd like to introduce you to three friends I had in my mind's eye as I assembled this material:

- Michael, a delivery truck driver and dynamic Christian, said to me, "Ken, I love Jesus, His Word, and the kids...do you think I can learn to be a good Bible teacher?" This brief conversation with Michael began his journey to becoming a highly effective Bible teacher and group leader. **Do you share Michael's passion, but feel the need to get some training before committing to teach?**

- My friend Dan, a graduate school professor, is a popular author and successful classroom lecturer. But Dan recognized that he needed new teaching tools to be a better teacher on Sunday morning. His group members at church were not responding in the way his grad students were. He eagerly embraced new approaches and became a better teacher in both settings. **Have you been teaching the Bible for a few years? Is the Holy Spirit prompting you to expand your repertoire of instructional techniques?**

- Jason, a local pastor, recently contacted me and described a significant faculty of dedicated teachers with whom he has frequent training sessions. Despite their regular and ongoing training, he recognized the teachers needed a fresh voice. Their teaching methods as a whole had plateaued, and his group needed to be challenged to a new level of performance. After engaging with these keys to teaching that transforms, his teachers have new insights and common terminology to inspire a change in culture in their Bible studies. **Are you responsible for the ongoing training of Bible study teachers and small group leaders at your church?**

If you can relate to one or more of these scenarios, this book is for you.

In each chapter...

- Key concepts of each chapter will be introduced, defined, and explained.
- Where possible, an example of the Key concept of that chapter from the *teaching of Jesus in the Gospels* will be presented side by side with that educational concept.
- Each of the Eight Keys is prominent in *21st century educational literature.* Brief snapshots of this research will be referred to, and you will be directed to additional sources for further reading and reflection.
- In the last ten years neuroscientists and educators have made significant connections between their discoveries in *"mind, brain, and education" research.* I share these findings as they are pertinent to how teenagers perceive, process, store, and communicate their understanding of new ideas.
- *Practical, but powerful, teaching techniques* that lead to meaningful engagement and authentic transformation will be described and illustrated. I want to assist you in developing a toolbox of new skills and techniques so you will be ready to put these into service at a moment's notice.

It is the author's belief, having met hundreds of teachers like yourself, that the Lord has given you a heart to serve Him and a desire to influence teenagers through the power of His Word. But just like Nathan, you are hungry for a deeper understanding about teaching and learning. Everyone who had a hand in the publication of this book believes these Eight Keys will open new insights about how your group members learn and change. Let's don't leave Nathan hanging. He needs our help to design meaningful Bible studies that glorify the Lord and contribute to the transformation of his teens.

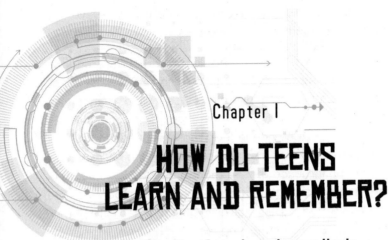

HOW DO TEENS LEARN AND REMEMBER?

Effective teachers know their students' brains don't have Velcro®!

Nathan's first attempt at leading the Bible study for his group of twenty teens went better than expected, given his anxiety just before he kicked off. He felt that he had researched the passage well and was prepared to answer background questions (which never came), but the teens never expressed any level of enthusiasm for the Scripture. He was thankful they cooperated and listened politely, but engaged, they were not. They were not rude or disinterested; they were passive...that's the word, they sat passively. Nathan expected more from them and more from himself. He needed to do some reading about teaching and learning.

Excellence in teaching God's Word is a critical component when developing a Bible teaching program that glorifies Christ, stimulates spiritual growth in believers, and ministers to both the members and the community God has called you to serve. The Apostle Paul said it best when he wrote and expressed his gratitude for the inspiring growth he saw in the saints at Thessalonica:

For this reason we also constantly thank God that when you received the word of God which you heard from us, you accepted it not as the word of men, but for what it really is, the

word of God, *which also performs its work in you who believe.*
1 Thessalonians 2:13 (emphasis added)

Paul points out that the believers at Thessalonica did not simply endorse him or embrace the message as coming from a human spokesperson. They took hold of his teaching for what it is, God's Word. Furthermore, he identified that it was already working in them. Paul communicates that the litmus test for excellence in teaching is the transformation of believers' lives by the power of the Holy Spirit. One of the major sources of this change is the influence of God's Word on an individual's thinking, believing, and behaving. Where there is effective teaching, there is *change*—in knowledge, in perspective, in attitudes, and ultimately, in behavior. *Where there is no change, no teaching and learning has occurred.* Yes, there can be passive consent, or short term memory of a set of facts. But long term, a lasting change in a person's life is necessary to say that teaching and learning has been successful and effective, and that God's word is "performing its work in you who believe."

With over thirty years' experience of teaching Bible study in many different contexts, this author has discovered that the key to seeing this change happen is the short, but powerful word, **engage**. Content that is taught with the use of techniques that offer the opportunity for Bible study participants to engage with God's Word, with the instructor, and with his/her classmates is more likely to take hold in the believer's mind and heart than instructional approaches in which the participants remain passive. Students learn more when they actively engage with the content than when they sit, listen, take notes, and watch. This book will reflect on the challenges and barriers to more effective teaching that exist in nearly every church and steps you and your fellow teachers/leaders can take to engaging your members in life-changing Bible study.

> **KEY #1: TRANSFORMATIONAL TEACHERS ASSIST THEIR STUDENTS IN THE PROCESS OF COMPREHENDING NEW INFORMATION AND BUILDING GOD'S TRUTH INTO THEIR THINKING AND BEHAVIOR.**

The big picture of what you are trying to accomplish:

Have you spent any time recently thinking about what you are hoping to accomplish when you teach a Bible study? Here are some possible responses from those who lead a group once a week:

- My goal is to cover the material.
- I try my best to communicate with my teens what I learned from my study of the passage.
- We have a curriculum especially designed for this age group that we try to get through each week and every quarter.
- We only have 45 minutes, and I try to pack it as full of Scripture as possible.
- After I explain the verses, I encourage my group to ask questions or share what it means to them.

How would you know or measure whether or not you accomplished your goal? The same teachers might respond:

- I was able to get through most of my notes.
- We spent some time on each of the verses we were supposed to cover.
- The teenagers appeared attentive and asked a few questions.
- On the way home in the car, my wife told me I did a good job teaching.

May I suggest that we as teachers of the Word of God, the most important truths in the universe, ought to set much higher expectations of ourselves? Consider these "big picture" goals—

- I would like for my students to fall more deeply in love with God's Word.
- My goal is for our teens to be able to study the Bible more effectively on their own.
- Each of us, when confronted with the truth of God's Word, should experience a change.
- I want our teens to be ready to give an account for the hope that is within them.

Developing a Philosophy of Teaching

At the outset of this book on teaching strategies, I want to encourage you to spend some time wrestling with your *philosophy of teaching and learning*. This is not the occasion for a deep discussion of this topic, but simply put, "what are your core beliefs about what you do as a teacher and how your students learn?" Though you may not realize it, this is an evaluation of your philosophy and your responses have a great deal to do with how you plan and carry out your Bible study lesson every week.

Most people, when they take a step back and look at themselves as teachers, will tell you they teach the way they do based on one of two things:

1. I teach the way my favorite teacher taught.
2. I teach the way I learn best.

While these responses may be both accurate and beneficial, I want to urge you to consider a third alternative—I teach in a variety of ways beneficial for the teens God has called me to lead and influence. Teaching is not about "ME," but it is focused on effectively communicating God's Word so teens are given the opportunity to interact with the biblical passage, with their leader, and with each other.

Would you like to change your approach to teaching? Do you need to add new tools to your tool belt that will inspire greater engagement during your Bible study?

This approach, dare I say, "this philosophy," focuses on what the students do and experience, not on what the teacher does or how much material is covered. A word of warning must be stated here. **While the teacher strongly considers what the students are doing and experiencing, God's Word remains the central focus; it is absolute and unchanging; its meaning is not constructed by the students individually or collectively.** But if you desire to see your students *change* (my one-word definition of *teaching and learning*), the teacher must develop strategies to **engage** them. Put another way, the teacher uses active learning techniques which challenge the student to interact with the content as opposed to **remaining passive while the instructor makes the presentation.**

This goes back to the theme of the lesson: *their brains are not made of Velcro®!* Teaching is not the act of throwing concepts at a surface to which they stick. Let's unpack this...during an instructional episode, the measure of whether or not teaching and learning took place is determined by to what extent did *change* take place in the students—change in perspective, attitude, values, disposition, understanding, but most important, change in behavior. We are exhorted by Scripture, "Don't just be hearers of the Word, but doers of the Word." The opportunity for change to take place in your students increases as they are engaged with the material, with the teacher, and with other learners. Why is this? Teaching and learning is NOT about the brilliance of the teacher or a truckload of material. It is about providing students with opportunities to construct their own understanding of the material.

Please read this carefully—I did **not** say "construct his/her own truth." With guidance from the Holy Spirit and the skillful leadership from a godly teacher, learners must have the opportunity to interact with the material in much the same way laborers work with building materials around them. The architect lays out the absolute dimensions of the project, beginning with the corner stone. He specifies the materials and design. Then the construction foreman oversees the brick layers or stone masons as they handle the building materials and construct the building. Our Bible study participants are not sponges that merely soak up material, nor are they like flypaper to which new material sticks. *They must be challenged to sort new ideas, to organize new thoughts, and find places to put them within their mental frameworks.* To fail to do this during the lesson is to miss significant opportunities for change and growth.

Throughout the Gospels we encounter Jesus engaging His disciples in the teaching–learning *process:*

Jesus engaged their imagination: "Consider the lilies of the fields."
Jesus engaged them in discussion: "Who do men say that I am?"
Jesus engaged them in problem solving: "Why are you troubled? Touch me and see..."

Jesus engaged them by connecting with their prior experience: "I am the bread of life."

Jesus engaged them with tests: "Whoever does not carry his own cross and come after me..."

Jesus engaged them in active learning: "You give them something to eat."

The central argument of this approach is that effective teaching is not the mere transmission of new ideas or dumping of course content, but as the examples above from Jesus' teaching illustrate, effective teaching includes the engagement of the learner. Christian author Gary Newton explains it this way:

> Learning is by nature active, interactive, and engaging. Even listening involves activity of the mind. Participants must discipline their thoughts, focus their attention, direct their gaze, and control their body language. Good listening skills involve all of these behaviors and activities. Learning happens most effectively through active engagement of every aspect of the person. The more engaged and active a person is in the learning process, the greater the potential for learning to take place.[1]

Authors Rick and Shera Melick agree with these two concepts of "change" and "engagement" and have crafted a unique term, *transformactional*. Here is how they summarize their understanding:

> Learning is more than mental. It is emotional. It is volitional. It is active. Transformation is indeed mental, but transformation also produces better living through informed action. In using the word "*transformactional*," we hope to stress two important aspects of learning. First, real learning includes action. Second, the process of learning is active. It actively seeks, embraces, and applies knowledge. In the case of Christian education, the learner actively seeks, embraces, and applies the truths of Scripture so that the learner develops Christ-like character and lifestyle.[2]

Some Christian educators shy away from the wording, *constructing knowledge*. Bassett and Baumann in *Foundations of Christian School*

Education write, "While a constructivist might say a learner '*builds meaning*' as he learns, a biblical Christian would be more comfortable saying that the learner '*discovers meaning*' or '*builds understanding*' of truths that already exist."[3]

As John Milton Gregory puts it in his classic book, *The Seven Laws of Teaching*, "Teaching is arousing and using the pupil's mind to grasp the desired thought or to master the desired art. Learning is thinking into one's own understanding a new idea or truth or working into habit a new art or skill."[4]

MacCullough refers to this as *interactive learning*—the process whereby the learner takes in new information from his or her surroundings and uses prior categories, vocabulary, and understandings to begin to process, make sense of, and store the information for retrieval and use. MacCullough presents four basic elements in an interactive teaching model:

Engaging the mind: activating the student's mind toward the topic of study.

Providing new information: giving new information or creating a student activity that requires the student to get it from an outside source.

Creating student processing activities: assisting students with opportunities to make connections with prior learning, draw conclusions, or practice a new skill.

Assessing learning: using student work products that represent the construction of their understanding as feedback on student achievement.[5]

Meaningful engagement that leads to transformational learning seldom occurs by accident, but can be a significant part of each instructional episode through systematic planning. This book will explore each of these ideas in upcoming chapters.

Significant ongoing studies known as "mind-brain-education" research has much to teach us as we close this chapter. As previously pointed out, Jesus demonstrated active learning techniques throughout His teaching ministry. In this century, neuroscientists now have the technology to trace what is occurring in a teenager's brain as he encounters new information and participates in instructional episodes. Author Judy Willis has the unique background of being both a neurologist and middle school teacher. She shares these insights regarding building strong memory circuits:

> Some of the strategies suggested by neuroimaging are ones that have students personalize information to be learned, thereby further activating the areas of the brain that help form memories... When students build their working memories through a variety of activities, they are stimulating multiple sensory intake centers in their brains. Their brains develop multiple pathways leading to the same memory storage destination. By stimulating several senses with the information, more brain connections are available when students need to recall that memory later on.[6]

Imagine your teens picking up new stuff that needs to be stored somewhere. So each one drives over to his/her storage unit and drops off the new gear. Willis and other educators point out that as teens learn multiple ways to drive over to the storage unit ("multiple pathways" in the above quote), they develop stronger connections to the new information. The result is that your group members will have greater recall of the new material. One of my favorite quotes from this research is, "*Cells that fire together, wire together*...When neurons fire in sync with one another, they are more likely to form new connections. As the connections grow stronger by repeated stimulation, a given neuron becomes more likely to trigger another connected neuron."[7]

The Power of a Nap...

As our teens experience intense periods of learning complex material (for example, a long sermon), they experience the depletion of chemicals vital to the memory retention process. (Neurotransmitters are necessary for the synapse process in storing new information.) Educators recommend a "syn-nap," pardon the pun. "Not only do these 'naps' prevent overloading of the circuits and interference with maximal memory storage conditions, but they also help maintain positive emotional states."[8]

Examples of activities could include the telling of a story related to the theme of the material or a two-minute break for group members to jot down notes or reflections regarding the new material. Other examples will be presented in chapter four.

>>>

Nathan's takeaway...

After spending time reflecting on his approach to presenting the material he gathered the previous week, Nathan was also determined to spend time preparing how he would shape the lesson. He decided it wasn't enough to create a well-organized package of new information and drop it on his twenty teens. They need more than that. The class deserves better than that. Nathan committed himself to learning how to engage his teenagers in the teaching–learning process with the expectation that transformation would take place.

<<<<<<<<<<<<<<<<<<<<<<<<<<<<<<<<<<<<<<<<<<<<<<<<<<<<<<<<<<<

Teacher Reflection:

1. Make a list of the teaching techniques used by instructors of classes where you learned the most. Reflect on this list based on the concepts of engagement presented in this chapter. Which methods required the greatest engagement? Which allowed you to remain passive?

2. Consider your overall goals for your current group or a future teaching opportunity? Did you include expectations for involving the participants or for assessing change in those who attend?

[1] Gary Newton, *Heart Deep Teaching: Engaging Students for Transformed Lives* (Nashville: B&H Academic, 2012), 107.

[2] Rick Melick and Shera Melick, *Teaching That Transforms: Facilitating Life Change Through Adult Bible Teaching* (Nashville: B&H Academic, 2010), 4.

[3] W. Philip Bassett and Eddie K. Baumann, "Teaching Methodologies," in *Foundations of Christian School Education: Perspectives on Christian Teaching*, eds. James Braley, Jack Layman, and Ray White (Colorado Springs: Purposeful Design Publications, 2003), 131.

[4] John Milton Gregory, *The Seven Laws of Teaching*, Rev. ed. (Mansfield Centre: Martino Publishing, 2011), 5.

[5] Martha A. MacCullough, *By Design: Developing a Philosophy of Education Informed by a Christian Worldview* (Langhorne: Cairn University, 2013), 100-101.

[6] Judy Willis, *Research-Based Strategies to Ignite Student Learning: Insights From a Neurologist and Classroom Teacher* (Alexandria: ASCD, 2006), 10.

[7] Ibid., 7.

[8] Ibid., 26-27.

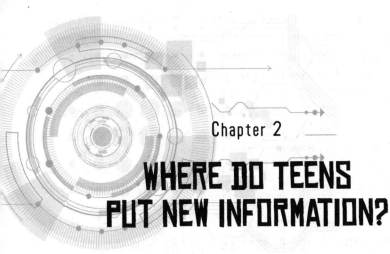

Chapter 2

WHERE DO TEENS PUT NEW INFORMATION?

**Effective teachers build on the
prior learning experience of their teens.**

*Nathan had always been inspired by Daniel chapter one.
He recalled important details about the exiles from Judah
being transported by conquerors over hundreds of miles as
he prepares to teach this passage to his youth group this
week. Four teens with odd names in a strange city found in a
civilization long since forgotten. What was God actually doing in the lives of these young men? More to the point—how
was Nathan supposed to get his group of kids to relate to the
passage of Scripture?*

Let's examine a brief but compelling encounter where we witness
Jesus' inspiring ability to connect with people, making use of the everyday ingredients of His listener's life. In Matthew chapter four, Jesus was
walking along the Sea of Galilee when He meets two brothers, Simon,
who was called Peter, and his brother Andrew. "They were casting a
net into the sea, since they were fishermen. 'Follow Me,' He told them,
'and I will make you fish for people!' Immediately they left their nets and
followed Him" (4:18-20, HCSB). Jesus was challenging Peter and Andrew
to a monumental change in their vocations and lifestyle, but He did so
using "a hook" and terminology with which they were familiar.

The instructional techniques of Jesus once again support and clarify current research. A modern educator need only consider the "I am" sayings of Jesus found in John's Gospel to recognize how Jesus connects with the general schema of disciples of all generations and cultures. All of mankind can grasp the temporal meanings of "bread of life," "the Good Shepherd," "the vine," or "the door." From the basis of these concrete pictures Jesus connects His listeners, past and present, to the eternal truth of His identity and His mission.

Early in my teaching career I would ask my audience to call to mind where they were when they heard that President Kennedy had been shot. As my career continued, I realized that many in my audience were too young to relate to the illustration. The question was greeted with a sea of blank stares. It was mandatory that the illustration be updated because I failed to connect with many of my younger group members. They lacked the prior knowledge or *schema* to relate to the historical reference in a meaningful way.

Gregory describes the importance of Nathan's concern in the scenario above in this description of the thinking–learning process—"It is painting in the mind of another the picture in one's own—the shaping of the thought and understanding to comprehension and of some truth which the teacher knows and wishes to communicate. The lesson to be mastered must be explicable in the terms of truth already known by the learner—the unknown must be explained by means of the known."[1] (emphasis added)

KEY #2: EFFECTIVE TEACHERS IDENTIFY THEIR GROUP MEMBERS' SCHEMA.

Definition: Schema—the prior understanding or knowledge a learner brings to a new learning episode. Jesus recognized He was teaching mind-boggling, life-changing concepts that ran counter to everything in the His learners' training and experience. He connected with their everyday experiences and His parables were not bound by first century culture.

Simplifying brain research on learning, we could say that a student picks up new ideas and asks, "Where do I put this? Do I have an existing file folder for this? If so, which file does this fit with? If not, do I really need this? So where does this fit?"

Two concerns arise related to students' use of new information and the construction of new concepts. Anderson and Krathwohl point out that research reveals many students do not make connections between what they learn in classrooms and their lives outside of school. "Students often seem to acquire a great deal of factual knowledge, but they do not understand it at a deeper level or integrate or systematically organize it in disciplinary or useful ways."[2]

A second concern is that students construct conceptions that "do not coincide with authentic aspects of reality or with well-accepted, normative conceptions of the information."[3] To state this another way, the students can misunderstand the correct meaning and reach conclusions that are simply wrong. These two issues highlight the importance of the educational concept in this chapter—each participant in your Bible study brings prior learning or lack thereof. This prior learning is called the learner's *schema*.

To summarize effective teaching skill #2:

Students learn more readily when they can connect what they are learning to what they already know. However, instructors should not assume that students will immediately or naturally draw on relevant prior knowledge. Instead, they should deliberately activate students' prior knowledge to help them forge robust links to new knowledge.[4]

By way of illustration, my wife grew up in a community in which she had never encountered the annual tradition of a "turkey shoot." After seeing announcements about Turkey Shoot Contests every year in my hometown, she finally asked me one day, "Ken, who wants the turkey after everyone has shot it?" My wife is very bright and had no difficulty identifying and pronouncing the words, *turkey shoot.* But she needed me to explain the concept of shooting at a target! In short, she had no prior experience or 'schema' for what she was reading. I suggest that every week in Bible study our group members are encountering the same experience—new terms and discussions for which they have no frame of reference.

Jesus demonstrates throughout the Gospels what recent educational research is verifying: "New knowledge sticks better when it has prior knowledge to stick to."[5]

One group of researchers explains the relationship between schema and new information this way:

> Students connect what they learn to what they already know, interpreting incoming information, and even sensory perception, through the lens of their existing knowledge, beliefs, and assumptions. In fact, there is widespread agreement among researchers that students must connect new knowledge to previous knowledge in order to learn. However, the extent to which students are able to draw on prior knowledge depends on the nature of their prior knowledge, as well as the instructor's ability to harness it.[6]

Two terms that are related to this discussion on knowledge development are *assimilation* and *accommodation*. Marzano points out that the ideas related to schema go back to Piaget's research on how children learn. *Assimilation* is the gradual integration of new knowledge into a learner's existing knowledge base. *Accommodation*, on the other hand, is a more significant change in that it involves creating new mental structures as opposed to simply adding to existing ones.[7]

Two concerns related to building on prior knowledge...

Insufficient prior knowledge...

One does not have to read far into the Gospels to identify Jesus' frequent quoting of the Mosaic Law, the Psalms, and Jewish history. His contemporaries were very familiar with these sources and traditions. However, today's Bible teacher may have to supply most of the biblical background information due to the overall unfamiliarity of teens with even the most famous of stories like the parting of the Red Sea, the fall of the walls of Jericho, and David versus Goliath. Another illustration of a teacher's concern with insufficient prior knowledge might be in the biblical concept of God as Heavenly Father. With a discouraging number of teens coming from families with no father in the home or even involved in the life of the teen, many attendees to a Bible study on the Lord's Prayer (Our Father, Who are in heaven....) might have no personal experience with their own biological fathers, or could even have a negative association with the term *father* or *fatherhood*.

Inaccurate prior knowledge...[8]

Sometimes the prior learning or experience that our teens bring to new information is just flat wrong and must be corrected. Here are three illustrations from the teaching of Jesus...

1) In the Gospel of John, chapter nine, Jesus and His disciples crossed paths with a blind man, which gave Jesus the perfect opportunity to correct a long standing misunderstanding in their Jewish culture regarding physical handicaps. Seeing the blind man, His disciples asked,

"Rabbi, who sinned, this man or his parents, that he would be born blind?"

Jesus answered, "*It was* neither *that* this man sinned, nor his parents; but *it was* so that the works of God might be displayed in him. We must work the works of Him who sent Me as long as it is day; night is coming when no one can work. While I am in the world, I am the Light of the world."

2) In Luke 7:36-50, Jesus accepted both the invitation of a Pharisee to join him for a meal as well as the poignant gift of a "woman of the city" who wet Jesus' feet with her tears and wiped them with her hair. Seeing Jesus accept her humble service, the Pharisee responded, "If this man were a prophet, he would have known who and what sort of woman this is who is touching him, for she is a sinner" (ESV). Once again, the downfall of applying inaccurate prior knowledge regarding our Savior.

3) In Luke 6:6-11, Jesus chose to directly confront the Pharisees' legalism about the Sabbath. Scripture says, "But he knew their thoughts, and he said to the man with the withered hand, 'Come and stand here.' And Jesus said to them, "I ask you, is it lawful on the Sabbath to do good or to do harm, to save life or to destroy it?" (ESV). Jesus proceeded to heal the man's hand and in so doing, infuriated the scribes and the Pharisees.

Dealing with inaccurate prior knowledge can be difficult and may best be dealt with by direct correction. As Ambrose and her co-authors describe the process: "However, some kinds of inaccurate prior knowledge—called *misconceptions*—are remarkably resistant to correction. Misconceptions are models or theories that are deeply embedded in students' thinking."[9] Paul's letter to the Galatians is an excellent example. His letter varies from biblical challenge (3:11— "now it is evident that no one is justified before God by the law, for 'The righteous shall live by faith'" (ESV)), to legal argument (3:15—"To give a human example, brothers: even with a man-made covenant, no one annuls it or adds to it once it has been ratified" (ESV)), to outright scolding (3:1-2—"O foolish Galatians! Who has bewitched you? It was before your eyes that Jesus Christ was publicly portrayed as crucified. Let me ask you only this: Did you receive the Spirit by works of the law or by hearing with faith?" (ESV)). This misconception persists today with many "believers" convinced that entrance into Heaven is based on having done more good acts than bad.

Dealing with these concerns related to prior learning...

In Luke 9:18-20 Jesus asks a fascinating question: "Who do men say that I am?" While Jesus certainly did not need to inquire of His disciples to get insights into the public's perception of His ministry, it did give them the opportunity to voice the misperceptions that others had about Him. (This will be explored in more detail in chapter seven of this text.) Here Jesus provides us with an excellent teaching technique to deal with insufficient or inaccurate prior learning. Give your group a brief quiz/evaluation and find out the extent of their knowledge so you can begin at the best place as you move forward in your teaching.

The Power of a Story...

Jesus frequently demonstrates the attention grabbing, life-changing influence of a well-placed story. Recall your favorite parables from the Gospels—the Good Samaritan, the Lost Sheep, or the Parable of the Sower. Each of these were magnificently designed to connect with the everyday affairs of His contemporaries and all people throughout time. These connections include all the areas of cognitive, emotional, and spiritual dimensions of human makeup. As you prepare each week, study your focal passage as early in your week as possible—I recommend reading the passage through at least once a full week before you teach. Then continue prayerfully to search for the most current, relevant story you can find to connect biblical truth to the lives of your teens.

Another Way to View Connection...

Gary Newton suggests that teachers of teens reflect on the needs of students as they prepare points of intersection between a biblical passage and their teens. He suggests these four categories of potential connection[10]:

- Cognitive: what will they be thinking as they read the passage? What vocabulary or theological wording will be difficult? What would confuse them?
- Affective: What might they be feeling? What emotional reactions would they have? Will any of the material be disturbing?
- Volitional: What questions or struggles will they encounter in the text?
- Behavioral: What practices or applications are a natural outgrowth of the study? Will teens find these difficult? Perhaps even unthinkable?

Mind, Brain, and Education Research...*Help Teens Remember!*

Judy Willis, who is both a neurologist and certified middle school teacher, makes a powerful argument for the concepts of this chapter when she writes,

Students can retain the new information by activating their previously learned knowledge that relates to the new material. This prior knowledge exists in stored loops of brain cell connections. Effective teaching uses strategies to help students recognize patterns and then make the connections required to process the new working memories so they can travel into the brain's long-term storage areas.[11]

So why be concerned about *connecting*?

Why be concerned about your group members' *schema*? The first and most obvious point is that you want to get their attention. We all know that no one is going to accompany you on a trip involving a new passage of Scripture unless you have their attention. The process is so much more than capturing a teen's attention, which could just as easily be done by a loud noise, outrageous behavior, or a humorous story.

- Connecting with their schema allows them to place the unknown next to the known.
- Connecting with their schema aids in the construction of understanding, as described in the previous chapter.
- Connecting with their schema facilitates storage of new information, perspectives, and attitudes.
- Connecting with their schema adds memory retention and retrieval of new insights.

Newton calls the practice of identifying and connecting with learners' schema "priming the pump." (Originally, this idiom referred to pouring liquid into a pump, which would expel the air and allow it to start. With the neuroscience research in mind, perhaps "light the fire" may be an even better metaphor for the concept of sparking your group's thinking.) Newton argues persuasively, "The introduction is the most important part of the lesson...The richer the priming experience, the more potential there is to draw water from the well of God's Word into the depths of the heart of the person."[12] His points about priming the pump include:

- It brings to the surface the needs of teens.
- It establishes a goal for the lesson.
- It encourages students to express where they are and what they know.
- It opens and softens the hearts of the students.
- It serves as a springboard, providing excitement and anticipation about the lesson.[13]

》》》

Nathan's takeaway...

What could this look like in Nathan's lesson plan for Daniel chapter one?

Here are some potential opening questions designed to connect his group members' prior experience to different dimensions of the biblical text. (Note: Your opening engagement doesn't necessarily have to transition immediately to the first point in your outline. Nor does it have to tie into what you have determined to be the number one takeaway from the passage.)

Setting—Have you ever been forced to move from your home, your school, your favorite team? What emotional reactions did you have to overcome?

Think of a place in which you encountered a radically different culture...the bright light of a big city with sights, sounds, and smells.

Characters—Do you have a posse you travel with? Is the peer pressure in a positive direction? How do you respond to a new teacher or coach giving you forceful instructions?

Theme—Has God challenged you to be different in a particular setting? If so, can you imagine glorifying Him as you select a lonely, harder path?

Conflict in the plot—Recall a situation when you were pressed to compromise your biblical commitments. Could your reaction to the situation be best described as *fight, flight,* or *paralysis*?

《《《

Teacher Reflection:

1. Review your most recent Bible studies and reflect on your approach to beginning the study. In addition to leading in prayer and reading the lesson passage, did you specifically plan something that would be a "hook" to catch their attention? To continue the metaphor, did they "take the bait?" Have you had the experience of saying to yourself, "This isn't working?" Reflecting

on these experiments and failures will make you a better teacher.

2. Perhaps you have become convinced as you worked through this chapter that you should strive diligently to connect with your students' prior learning and experience, but you are finding you just don't know how. Even if you limit your research to just the time you spend at Bible study, you should pick up many new insights. You can do this by being a good listener as you engage them during class...writing, illustrating, talking to another group member. And that's just during the lesson. Try following them on social media and you'll really find out what's important to them.

---

[1] John Milton Gregory, *The Seven Laws of Teaching*, Rev. ed. (Mansfield Centre: Martino Publishing, 2011), 2.

[2] Lorin W. Anderson et al., eds. *A Taxonomy for Learning, Teaching, and Assessing: A Revision of Bloom's Taxonomy of Educational Objectives* (Addison Wesley Longman, Inc., 2001), 42.

[3] Ibid., 38.

[4] Susan A. Ambrose et al., *How Learning Works: Seven Research-Based Principles for Smart Teaching* (San Francisco: Jossey-Bass, 2010), 18.

[5] Ibid., 15.

[6] Ibid.

[7] Robert J. Marzano, *The Art and Science of Teaching: A Comprehensive Framework for Effective Instruction* (Alexandria: ASCD, 2007), 59.

[8] Ambrose, *How Learning Works*, 23.

[9] Ibid., 24.

[10] Gary Newton, *Heart-Deep Teaching: Engaging Students for Transformed Lives* (Nashville: B&H Publishing Group, 2012), 88. .

[11] Judy Willis, *Research-Based Strategies to Ignite Student Learning: Insights From a Neurologist and Classroom Teacher* (Alexandria: ASCD, 2006), 6.

[12] Newton, *Heart-Deep Teaching*, 152.

[13] Ibid., 153-156.

Chapter 3

DOES SITTING PASSIVELY AND LISTENING PROMOTE ANYTHING MORE THAN NAPPING?

Effective teachers engage their learners.

Nathan was excited about the breakthroughs in his lesson planning and delivery. He was following a curriculum resource that included 2 Corinthians chapter one for the upcoming week. As was his practice, he began early in the week to read and reread the passage to begin the process of praying through the main ideas of the passage. Nathan contacted members of the group and talked through the major theme of the chapter hoping he could get some ideas about thought-provoking ways to engage his kids. He was amazed at what they came up with!

With over thirty years' experience teaching Sunday School in three different locations, I have discovered the key to students' learning is the short, but powerful word, **engage**. Throughout the lesson effective teachers look for ways to engage students with God's Word, with the instructor, and with his/her classmates. Content taught with techniques that offer the opportunity for Bible study participants to engage is more likely to take hold in the believer's mind and heart than instructional approaches in which the participants remain passive. Students learn more when they actively engage with the content than when they sit, listen, take notes, and watch the teacher. In a conversation with Dr. Johnny Hunt, pastor of First Baptist Church, Woodstock, Georgia, and his minister of education, Allan Taylor, both experienced leaders agreed—this is exactly what is needed in Bible study groups today. They were not saying lecturing is a poor way to teach, but they strongly stated that lecture by itself for the entirety of the Sunday School hour is not getting the job done.

Popular author and experienced teacher Robyn Jackson expressed her philosophy this way in her book *Never Work Harder Than Your Students and Other Principles of Great Teaching*: "One day, in the midst of a particularly boring worksheet I looked at their glazed over faces and realized that while they were now compliant, they were not learning a thing. At that point, I came face to face with my values. Was it more important that my students be quiet and cooperative, or was it more important that they *actively engage* (emphasis mine) with the material and learn to be critical thinkers and effective communicators? Was it more important that I feel in control of the classroom, or was it more important that my students learn?"[1]

KEY #3: EFFECTIVE TEACHERS ENGAGE THEIR LEARNERS.

Engagement is possible in a variety of ways through the use of *Active Learning Techniques* during your lesson. In *Teaching Strategies: A Guide to Effective Instruction*, Donald Orlich and his coauthors define *active learning* as "a wide range of teaching strategies that engage the learner in the actual instruction that takes place. Seat-work is passive. Students working on problems in small groups (are) active.... An active learning classroom is a learning community where all participate, including the teacher.[2]

Jesus Modeled Engagement...

Following the most significant event in all of history, the resurrection of our Savior, His disciples were struggling mightily to process the recent events. Luke 24:36-53 tells us the eleven were together talking, and Jesus suddenly stood in their midst. He knew their mind set and emotional upheaval—"they were startled and frightened and thought they saw a spirit" (verse 37, ESV). Having gotten their attention, Jesus provided them with two experiments allowing them the opportunity to gather information that would lead to the truth. First, He invited them to have a tactile experience that would contradict what their hypothesis stated—that He was a spirit or ghost—"Touch me, and see. For a spirit does not have flesh and bones as you see that I have" (verse 39, ESV). Second, He conducted another experiment and further engaged His disciples—"Have you anything to eat?" (verse 41, ESV). "They gave him a piece of broiled fish, and he took it and ate before them" (verse 42-43, ESV). According to this description in Luke, not until Jesus engaged His disciples in the new learning experience did He begin to describe what had just happened and the coming events. He knew His followers were not in an emotional state of readiness to listen to a discourse on the resurrection body.

What actually happens in a Bible study when teachers engage their students the way Jesus did in the passage from Luke? First, the learner actually participates in the construction of a new perspective in his mind. He has fresh experiences in organizing and evaluating his thoughts and beliefs about a topic. Research shows that students learn much more by doing things and getting feedback than by watching someone and listening to someone tell them what they're supposed to know.[3]

Second, the learner, as a participant, should perceive that the teacher or a classmate actually values what he or she has to offer. This builds confidence and reinforces for the learner that his or her contribution really matters.[4]

As this narrative in Luke demonstrates, Jesus cared deeply about His disciples and about their accurate comprehension of His identity and their role in His mission.

On almost every page of the Gospels, Jesus demonstrated effective teaching methods for us to follow. The previous discussion of Luke 24 illustrates magnificently the teaching methodology known as the *5Es*, an approach that evolved through several iterations throughout the 20th century. Let's examine Luke 24 through the framework of the *5Es*:

Engage: Jesus appears to His disciples without entering through the door. He certainly captures their attention and curiosity! Their prior hunches about what a ghost is like enters their minds.

Explore: Jesus provided them the opportunity to carry out two experiments. This step builds on step one—they had several fears and hypotheses and now they get to test them.

Explain: The disciples may have been discussing their findings as they observed and reflected on the data. Rather than presenting a lecture on His Resurrection Body, Jesus gave them the opportunity to reflect on their experiences and refine their thoughts.

Elaboration: Verse 45 states, "Then he opened their minds to understand the Scriptures." Following their tactile experiences with His wounds and the fish, they were prepared to listen with calm, focused minds to fresh insights about His identity and purpose.

Evaluate: Jesus often conducted brief assessments. In the case of the disciples, they met with Jesus again before His ascension, and He would test Peter in particular. See John 21.5

Mind, Brain, and Education Research...

The following insights from current research have many implications for how we engage our teens in the process of discipleship:

Engaging in the process of learning actually increases one's capacity to learn. Each time a student participates in any endeavor, a certain number of neurons are activated. When the action is repeated, such as when performing a follow-up lab experiment or rehearsing a song, these same neurons respond again. The more times one repeats an action or recalls the information, the more dendrites sprout to connect new memories to old, and the more efficient the brain becomes in its ability to retrieve that memory or repeat that action.[6]

What does engagement look like?

Two authors, Michael Opitz and Michael Ford, discuss the close connection between the all-important need for students to be motivated and the teacher's need to engage students in the learning process. They maintain that engagement indicates the learner is involved and engrossed in encountering new ideas. However, they stress three conditions must be present: participants feel they can be successful, they value the outcome from the task at hand, and they feel safe in the learning environment.[7] Citing the work of Philip Schlechty, Opitz and Ford describe engaged learners as follows:

Attentive: Participants are focused on the activity.

Committed: Participants willingly work to complete the task without extrinsic reward or threat of sanction.

Persistent: Participants stay engaged when the task becomes difficult.

Meaning seekers: Participants find value in the completion of the activity.[8]

Engage through Active Learning Techniques (ALTs)...

As previously stated, learners stay focused better when they are actively involved in the lesson as opposed to listening passively to a lecture. And merely asking, "Does anyone have any questions?" does not count as discussion or participation. Teachers need to be challenged to plan intentionally to design participation opportunities in their lesson plans. This is not to say that any lecture is a poor second to active learning. What needs to take place is a balance between the teacher presenting the information that has been researched prior to class with episodes in which the class members interact with the teacher, the Scripture, and each other. A teacher who is new to this approach might set a goal of making use of two ALTs each lesson, placing new ones at different places in the lesson each week. As both the teacher and the class become familiar with new expectations, the number of ALTs per lesson could increase to three or four activities each week. Besides, an ALT can take as little time as it takes for class members to show their response after considering a question and giving it a "thumbs up" or a "thumbs down." Fifteen seconds!

The following categories of active learning techniques are intended to present some specific approaches. Also, the categories are presented in a format that suggest an ever-increasing level of engagement, from thinking (and no movement) to highly involved engagement that includes physical movement around the classroom and interaction with other students. In addition, as the suggested activities increase in their level of engagement, they also increase in the amount of instructional time it takes to employ the technique.

Thinking: The teacher invites the students to imagine a specific situation or call to their mind's eye a picture or memory. The teacher does so in an effort to connect with a prior experience that may include an emotional connection. While no movement or conversation is required, the learner has the opportunity to become more engaged than simply listening passively. For example, the Bible study teacher can invite students to think back to a recent confrontation that required them to exercise *agape* love in the interaction with another person. At this level of engagement, no verbal responses are requested and the engagement requires only a brief amount of time. (This approach takes the least amount of time and involves no physical movement. As both student and teacher exert greater energy and more time, engagement increases. With the increase of energy and time the learner builds deeper understanding and greater change can take place.)

Reading: Interacting with printed text is crucial in most every discipline, but particularly in Bible study. Every class session or group meeting should include reading God's Word either aloud or silently, or both. But often students do not remain focused while reading any given passage. *Read with a Purpose* is an approach that engages students, holds their attention, and assists in constructing new insights.

> **Step one:** The teacher leads a brief discussion that is related to both the students' schema and a major point in the text they are about to read.
>
> **Step two:** The teacher poses a question related to the text and asks the students to look for one or more specific ideas while the text is read aloud or silently.

Step three: The teacher asks students to present their responses to the question in step two. As he/she gages their level of understanding, the teacher can probe for deeper insights.

Step four: The teacher, depending on the readiness of the group, then assigns additional reading, usually longer than the first portion in step two. Once again, the teacher poses one or more questions and asks the students to think about them as they read.

Writing: this ALT is an excellent place for metacognitive reflection (chapter five) and formative assessment (chapter seven). The one-minute paper is a popular approach that is most often used at the conclusion of an instructional episode. The teacher requests that all students, using a notecard or half-sheet of paper, record what they believe to be the most important point(s) in the lesson. Another approach is called "The Muddiest Point" essay—students are asked to describe a point in the lesson that was confusing to them and if possible, explain in what way the material or presentation was perplexing. One other idea is to encourage students to write random ideas or reactions on easel paper posted around the room. The comments need not be tightly organized or formatted a certain way. Thus, the technique is called, Graffiti Board.[9]

Interaction between students nearby:

Think-pair-share. Pose the problem and have students work on it individually for a short time (usually 60 seconds). Next have them form pairs and reconcile and improve their solutions. Finally call on several individuals or pairs to share their responses. This structure takes a bit more time than a simple group activity, but it includes individual thinking and leads to greater learning.

Thinking-aloud pair problem solving (TAPPS). This is a powerful technique for helping students work through and understand a problem solution, case analysis, text interpretation, or translation. Have the students get into pairs and designate one pair member as the explainer and the other one as the questioner. Give the explainers a minute or two to explain the problem statement line by line (explain the first paragraph of the case history, interpret, or translate the first paragraph of the text) to their partners. Tell the questioners to ask questions when explanations are unclear or incomplete and to give hints when necessary. Stop the students after the allotted time (usually no more than three minutes) and call on several individuals to explain things to you. Once you get a satisfactory explanation, have the pairs reverse roles and continue with the next part of the problem solution, case analysis, text interpretation, or translation. Proceed in this manner until the exercise is complete. In the end, your students will understand the exercise material to an extent that no other instructional technique we know of can match.[10]

The Power of a One-on-One Conversation...

If you have an upcoming international mission trip or a cross-cultural teaching opportunity, you should strongly consider the think-pair-share approach to student engagement. I have done so in the last few years in Haiti, Cuba, Panama, and the Democratic Republic of the Congo (DRC). Though my new friends were apprehensive at first, I challenged audiences to have brief, focused conversations about the new teaching concepts I was presenting. Adult participants in these cultures have grown up in an educational system that focuses on "the sage on stage," but they were delighted to have the opportunity to engage in short conversations with their "elbow partner." Both the teacher and the participants found this to be a very productive use of time.

Movement Around the Room:

Tea Party: The teacher prepares several questions connected to the lesson that group members respond to without preparation. As class members enter, hand each one a card that contains instructions to consider his/her response to one of the questions. After each student thinks about a response, he/she should find someone with a different colored card (containing a different question). Each person should read his/her question and share a response. Repeat as time permits.

Gallery Walk: This technique follows a cooperative group activity during which group members recorded their thoughts on easel paper. (This work product is usually significant and has too many ideas to be presented orally in class.) All groups post their paper on the walls of the classroom and students are given time to browse around the room, much the same as one does at an art gallery. If necessary, each group leaves behind one member to serve as a guide to answer questions.

Post-It Note®: Each group member responds to a question or challenge by writing a response on a Post-It Note®. Students are asked to stick his/her response in the appropriate category on the board.

A Five Step Approach to Engaging Your Teens...

A familiar approach to teaching is called *chunk and chew*—dividing content into bite-sized pieces and providing your group time to think through and digest the new information. At the core of this technique is the notion that piling on new concepts upon new concepts doesn't lead to strengthening teens' comprehension. It also emphasizes giving them time to engage with the material. Recently this method has expanded to include additional steps:

> **Chunk:** Present new content in segments lasting no more than ten minutes.
>
> **Challenge:** The teacher presents a question or task that encourages deeper exploration of the passage.
>
> **Chew:** Students have as little as 30 seconds or 2-3 minutes to engage with new ideas. During this time, they begin formulating how to express the truth of the lesson.
>
> **Chat:** A beneficial way to express new ideas is to have informal conversations with peers or with the leader.
>
> **Check:** At the conclusion of the study, the teacher can lead a full group discussion to evaluate the group's understanding or ask participants to respond individually in writing.[11]

Below is a summary of the ideas presented in this chapter. When given the opportunity to be engaged during a Bible study, the learner has the opportunity to experience:

- Active responses, as opposed to passive consideration
- Construction of concepts, as opposed to simple review of another's definition
- Higher-order thinking, as opposed to mere recognition of a process or a concept
- Assessment, as opposed to tacit acceptance

- Use of prior experience, as opposed to collection of new concepts that can be pushed aside for sorting later
- Hearing what he or she has constructed (another experience in organizing and evaluating)
- Perceiving that the teacher and/or classmates actually value what he or she has to offer
- Movement and responses (physiological change) that create a new sense of energy in the room
- Competition that creates heightened awareness and, in some cases, increased learning
- Use of formative assessment to enhance his or her self-evaluation

〉〉〉

Nathan's takeaway...

His students dug into the assigned passage, 2 Corinthians 1:3-7, and discovered that our English word *comfort* and its various forms are used ten times. With a little more digging they learned the Greek word for *comfort* is *paraklesis*.[12] With apologies for the bad play on words, they decided to call all their friends and ask them to wear a pair of athletic shoes that have cleats...so everyone had on a "pair-a-cleats." The value of the engagement was deepened as they discussed the qualities of a worthwhile pair of cleats—comfort in all situations and able to provide gripping power or endurance—two of the key points of the passage. Nathan could not have been more thankful for his senior leaders and their lesson plan ideas that engaged the group in memorable ways.

〈〈〈

Teacher Reflection:

1. Which of the two lesson outlines do you prefer that were presented in this chapter?
   The 5Es: Engage, Explore, Explain, Elaborate, and Evaluate...
   Or

The 5 Step Chunk & Chew: Chunk, Challenge, Chew, Chat, and Check...

Share your choice with a partner and discuss why your selection fits your teaching style.

2. Have you noticed your teens exhibiting a drop in energy or decrease in focus as you teach? Select three of the Active Learning Techniques presented in this chapter that you would be comfortable using without any prior preparation—save these as methods that you could pull out and use when you need to. For practice, look over the last lesson that you taught and reflect on when and how you could have used the three ALTs you selected.

---

[1] Robyn R. Jackson, *Never Work Harder Than Your Students and Other Principles of Great Teaching* (Alexandria: ASCD, 2009), 93.

[2] Donald C. Orlich et al., *Teaching Strategies: A Guide to Effective Instruction* (Boston: Wadsworth, 2010), 40.

[3] Michael Prince, "Does Active Learning Work? A Review of the Research," *J. Engr. Education* 93, no. 3, pg. 229 (July 2004), http://www4.ncsu.edu/unity/lockers/users/f/felder/public/Papers/Prince_AL.pdf (accessed July 20, 2016), quoted in Richard M. Felder and Rebecca Brent, "Active Learning: An Introduction," *ASQ Higher Education Brief* 2, no. 4, pg. 3 (August, 2009), http://www.smith.edu/sherrerdcenter/docs/ALpaper(ASQ).pdf (accessed July 21, 2016).

[4] Robert J. Marzano, Debra J. Pickering, and Jane E. Pollock, *Classroom Instruction That Works: Research-Based Strategies for Increasing Student Achievement* (Alexandria: ASCD, 2001), 50, 85.

[5] Tracey Tokuhama-Espinosa, *Making Classrooms Better: 50 Practical Applications of Mind, Brain, and Education Science* (New York: W. W. Norton & Company, Inc., 2014), 218.

[6] Judy Willis, *Research-Based Strategies to Ignite Student Learning: Insights From a Neurologist and Classroom Teacher* (Alexandria: ASCD, 2006), 8.

[7] Michael F. Opitz and Michael P. Ford, *Engaging Minds in the Classroom: The Surprising Power of Joy* (Alexandria: ASCD, 2014), 17.

[8] Philip C. Schlechty, *Engaging Students: The Next Level of Working on the Work* (San Francisco: Jossey-Bass, 2011) in Michael F. Opitz and Michael P. Ford, *Engaging Minds in the Classroom: The Surprising Power of Joy* (Alexandria: ASCD, 2014), 18.

[9] Andrea M. Guillaume, Ruth Helen Yopp, and Hallie Kay Yopp, *50 Strategies For Active Teaching: Engaging K-12 Learners In The Classroom*, Merrill/Prentice

Hall Teaching Strategies Series (Upper Saddle River, N.J.: Pearson Merrill Prentice Hall, 2007), 81.

[10] Richard M. Felder and Rebecca Brent, "Active Learning: An Introduction," *ASQ Higher Education Brief* 2, no. 4, pg. 3 (August, 2009), http://www.smith.edu/sherrerdcenter/docs/ALpaper(ASQ).pdf (accessed July 21, 2016).

[11] Emily Mather, "Chunk-Challenge-Chew-Chat-Check," *Education Update* 57, no. 6, pg. 7 (June, 2015), http://www.ascd.org/publications/newsletters/education_update/jun15/vol57/num06/Chunk-Challenge-Chew-Chat-Check.aspx (accessed July 21, 2016).

[12] Geoffrey W. Bromiley, *Theological Dictionary of the New Testament*, Abridged in One Volume, eds. Gerhard Kittel and Gerhard Friedrich (Grand Rapids: William B. Eerdmans Publishing Company, 1985), 778.

Chapter 4

DO TEENS ALL LEARN THE SAME WAY?

Effective teachers recognize and respond to the need for diversity in their approaches.

Nathan was getting more comfortable with his new approach to engaging his group members, but recognized that two or three teens were not focused and committed to some of the Active Learning Techniques he had been using. Thankfully none of the culprits were distracting or discouraging other group members. The lesson for this coming week came from 1 Corinthians, and he was planning to drill down on Paul's theme on divisions in the church. This concept was just too important to have a misfire. He decided to meet with one of the older members of the group and kick around some ideas for designing ALTs that would inspire the maximum number of participants.

I love watching dramas that include crime scene investigators. It's fascinating to look over the shoulder of a veteran detective who knows what he is looking for when he enters a room full of clues. How about you, when you face a room full of teenagers? Are you picking up on all the clues the group is giving you about how they learn? First, do you think they learn just like you do? Second, do you think they all learn alike? This chapter will help you take the initial steps to reading the clues in your group.

Put another way, when it comes to designing teaching activities, "One size doesn't fit all."[1] Would you order an extra-large shirt for everyone in your group in preparation for your next outing? Ridiculous... most won't fit. They would look bad. Some students would refuse to wear them. But let's be honest—we approach our teaching that way! Because our group members sit passively and even cooperate, we interpret their behavior as approval on their part and effective teaching on the part of the teacher.

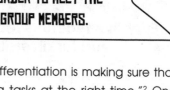

KEY #4: DIFFERENTIATION MEANS MAKING USE OF DIFFERENT TECHNIQUES IN ORDER TO MEET THE DIVERSE NEEDS OF YOUR GROUP MEMBERS.

One teacher explains it this way: "Differentiation is making sure that the right students get the right learning tasks at the right time."[2] One expert describes this approach as: "A differentiated classroom provides different avenues to acquiring content, to processing or making sense of ideas, and to developing products so that each student can learn effectively."[3]

Effective teaching requires the instructor do more than present content in a fashion he finds appealing to himself. It requires extraordinary effort, creativity, and training on behalf of the teacher for every student to grasp and integrate into his thinking and life the key concepts of the instructional episode.

Let's check out what Scripture says ...

Paul captures this theme of *differentiation* when he states, "We proclaim Him, admonishing every man and teaching every man with all wisdom, so that we may present every man complete in Christ. For this purpose also I labor, striving according to His power, which mightily works within me" (Colossians 1:28-29). First, teachers who differentiate their instructional techniques acknowledge the differences that exist from one learner to another. It is instructive to notice the repetition of the phrase *every man* in the verses above. Paul was driven to communicate Christ to every individual with whom he came in contact. The universality of the Gospel is captured in the plural form *every*. Teachers who differentiate believe most students can learn most things that are essential to a given area of study.[4]

The individual and unique nature of each recipient of Paul's message is indicated by Paul's use of the singular form of *man*.[5] The teacher who differentiates believes "each student should have equity of access to excellent learning opportunities."[6]

Second, Paul states in verse 29 that this pursuit requires arduous effort. The term Paul uses for our word *labor* indicates weariness and exertion.[7] The Greek word that follows (translated here as *striving*) was used frequently by Paul and referred to competing in athletic contests in his day, (translated *struggling* in other versions.)[8]

Paul's approach to "admonishing and teaching" was neither casual nor dispassionate. Unlike the popular concept of teaching as being "the sage on stage," Paul describes his interaction with the saints at Colossae as grueling work.

A closer look at the word *admonishing* gives us another indication of why his approach to teaching was so exhausting. "This verb 'admonish,' 'warn,' or 'instruct' had to do with setting the mind of someone in proper order, correcting him or putting him right."[9]

Wright describes the concept of *nouthetountes* this way:

> Though sometimes understood as meaning simply 'putting into the mind', most likely it includes the idea of setting of someone's mind into proper order, with the implication that it has been in some way out of joint. Positive teaching may not be enough: there is no telling what muddles Christian minds will get into from time to time, and part of the task of one who proclaims Christ is to straighten out confusions, to search for and correctly tie together the loose ends of half-grasped ideas, so that the positive teaching may not be instantly distorted upon reception, but may be properly understood, appreciated and lived out.[10]

In this analysis of the Greek word for *admonition* O'Brien intersects with two additional concepts discussed later in this lesson: the teacher's awareness of the learner's *schema* and the importance of the teacher paying attention to metacognitive processes. Each will be examined in more detail and connected to the overall theme of active engagement in the teaching/learning process.

What Do You Believe About Your Group Members? Before making modifications in your teaching based on the notion of participant differences, let's examine what Scripture has to say about the teens the Holy Spirit has guided to your group. (This list is a modification of a similar list from Tomlinson, pp. 27-35. What appears in bold is an exact quote from the book. The biblical discussion that follows is a modification of her argument.)

Belief 1: Every student is worthy of dignity and respect.

God's Word is crystal clear on this. Ephesians 2:10 states: "For we are His workmanship, created in Christ Jesus for good works, which God prepared in beforehand so that we would walk in them." The word translated here workmanship is *poiema* in the original language. This Greek word gives us our English term *poetry*. Challenge every member of your community to view each teen as God's poetry, His craftsmanship, His masterpiece.

Belief 2: Diversity is both inevitable and positive.

Paul carefully describes the benefits and beauty of diversity in 1 Corinthians 12:4-20. "Now there are varieties of gifts, but the same Spirit; and there are varieties of service, but the same Lord; and there are varieties of activities, but it is the same God who empowers them all in everyone...But as it is, God arranged the members in the body, each one of them as he chose. If all were a single member, where would the body be? As it is, there are many parts, yet one body" (ESV). So rather than struggling with meeting a variety of learner needs, Paul's exhortation is that we embrace and celebrate them.

Belief 3: The classroom should mirror the kind of society in which we want our students to live and lead.

In your youth group meetings and Bible studies, you are training the next generation of church leaders and teachers. They will probably be just like you! Once again, Paul challenges us, "Speaking the truth in love, we are to grow up in every way into him who is the head, into Christ, from whom the whole body, joined and held together by every joint with which it is equipped, when each part is working properly, makes the body grow so that it builds itself up in love" (Ephesians 4:15-16, ESV). Notice Paul's emphasis on "each part is working properly" and the process of growth, repeated twice. What a great picture of what we are called to do.

So what needs to be differentiated? Throughout this book there is an underlying theme that accompanies the major emphasis on engagement. This secondary theme is the need for differentiation. In each chapter, there are examples of Active Learning Techniques, none of which will be the one best approach to reach *every* teen in your group. But even the newest adult leader recognizes differences in maturity levels, reading comprehension ability, spiritual maturity, and biblical knowledge. Such disparate qualities can be frustrating and even frightening at times. Remember Bible study time can be incredible moments of building relationships and fostering transformation for all participants.

Carol Ann Tomlinson, one of the foremost authorities in the country on this topic, has established four major areas that deserve careful consideration for each group meeting:[11]

Your meeting environment: Variety in the physical environment is helpful when options such as furniture (types and arrangement), lighting (natural and electric), and temperature can be made available. The emotional environment is even more significant. Group members need to sense a welcoming, accepting atmosphere in which their differences are not only tolerated, but actually embraced as a valuable part of the group's learning process. As new attendees are engaged in teaching episodes, they sense that their ideas and perspectives are valued. Over time each participant recognizes his/her unique strengths are considered as groups are formed and tasks are performed.

Your content: Each time I lead a Bible study I consider the material from three dimensions of learning: Knowledge, Skills, and Dispositions (Know-Do-Be). I ask two simple questions regarding the designated passage for that lesson: What are the essential knowledge, skills, and spiritual attitudes each participant can learn and which concepts need to be acquired by all participants? Sometimes it is necessary to make strategic adjustments to accommodate learning needs of your participants. For example, ask this question, "While I have high expectations that all in attendance can grasp the big ideas of the lesson, how might

I adjust unfamiliar vocabulary to avoid unnecessary barriers?" Once a new point of theology is taught and discussed, perhaps the sophisticated vocabulary terms can be connected to it later in the unit of study.

Your teaching methods: In what ways can you engage every participant in your group, while being aware of the multitude of learning differences? Here's a question to be asked of the adult leaders in your ministry: Do you have two or more children at home? Do all of your children grasp new information in the same way? I have asked this question to thousands of parents and the majority respond without hesitation, "No, each of my children has a very unique learning style all his own." So if kids who come from the same gene pool and who grow up in the same environment have unique styles and preferences, why should we think every participant in a youth group will be just alike? Here's an achievable goal: at least once a month I will include a strategy in my lesson plan that highlights each participant's preference for encountering and working with new information. Here is a partial list for today's teens:

- Use of technology and social media.
- The opportunity to problem solve in a group.
- A few quiet moments to reflect without interaction or interruption.
- The chance to create something new—alone or in a group.
- The challenge to determine how I plan to use new information.
- The occasion to hear conflicting ideas and test my own beliefs.
- The chance to be successful at a task to build my confidence.

Your assessments/evaluations: We will discuss evaluating your group members' comprehension and progress in spiritual transformation in chapter seven, but for now it needs to be emphasized that teens should be given a wide variety of opportunities and assessment formats to evaluate understanding and growth. In general, we can agree that very little evaluation actually takes place in a local church. One exception may be rating elementary age children on Scripture memory. Some students better express their understanding in small group discussion, others in writing, and some through their actions. Check out the "Exit Ticket" idea in chapter seven—those teens who would never raise a question or share a different perspective have deep reservoirs of imagination and cognitive ability. Submitting a notecard as they leave the study may open up amazing creativity you didn't know was there.

Mind, Brain, and Education Research...

Multiple stimulations mean better memory—the more regions of the brain that store data about a subject, the more inter-connection there is. This redundancy means students will have more opportunities to pull up all those related bits of data from their multiple storage areas in response to a single cue. This cross-referencing of data strengthens the data into something we've learned rather than just memorized.[12]

Transformational teaching...illustrations of differentiation in process and product:

Making use of artistic abilities and the value of movement:

"And you were dead in your trespasses and sins..." (Ephesians 2:1-3). Begin by explaining the original meaning of *trespasses* (going out of bounds) and *sins* (missing the mark or target). Explain that our decisions against God's standards lead to separation and death.

Next, create groups of four students and allow each group to assign participants to these roles:

1) An artist
2) A volunteer to "play dead"
3) Medical examiner 1—a note taker
4) Medical examiner 2—presenter of the final product

Next, give each group a large sheet of paper and a marker that can be used to trace a silhouette of participant #2. As the artist traces this "crime scene" outline, the group can begin discussing types of evidence that is located within and around the outline. Making use of the imaginary evidence, the group writes a brief report as crime scene investigators would. (For example, material found on the shoes can give evidence of walking "out of bounds.")

Making use of dramatic abilities and the value of team competition:

Is learning books of the Bible important to you? If so, here's an Active Learning Technique that will assist your group members in creating great memories. Technique: Line Up.

Depending on the number of books in your study and the size of your group, divide the group in half and create a team competition. Assign one book to each participant. Each member must develop a sign or dramatic motion to represent his/her book. One participant from each team leaves the room while the groups practice. One option is to permit each team to have a drama coach. Before the missing member returns, the actors in each team are mixed up, out of order. No talking once the competition begins! Once the missing members return, the teams compete to see which group is placed in the correct order the fastest by their selected member.

Challenging higher order problem solving skills:

Research strongly supports the importance of giving students the opportunity to organize their thoughts by using graphic representations. One well known example of this is a Venn diagram which group members sort ideas into two categories: similarities and differences. For example, if your group were studying the parables from John that deal with God reaching out to lost people, students could decide which pieces of each parable are like the other two and which pieces are different.

The Power of a Post-It Note®:

Many teens are attentive and engaged, but lack the confidence and public speaking skills to express their thoughts to a large group of peers. Differentiate your approach to eliciting their commitment by distributing a Post-It Note® to each participant and ask for his/her response. If the Bible study was about forgiveness, ask each teen to jot down a brief description (no names) of someone that he/she needs to forgive. At the close of the study, each person voluntarily posts their note on a wall, easel, or whiteboard as an indication of a commitment to apply the Scripture to a real need.

But My Students Aren't Ready to Participate in Activities Like This...

At a recent educators' conference, I heard a seasoned teacher make these recommendations on how to coach up your group members so they can develop the needed skills to carry out some of the ALTs we are suggesting:

Steps for Successful Implementation of Active Learning Techniques—
Start Small: Begin with brief ALTs, perhaps 30-60 seconds.
Start Smart: Design ALTs that all group members can do and will find relevant.
Start Skills: Scaffold the skills you want to see developed.
Start Secure: Plan initial ALTs that won't isolate or embarrass your introverts.
Start Slow: Include one or two ALTs in your early lesson plans.
But Start! Don't let uncertainty prevent you from initiating your first attempts.[13]

〉〉

Nathan's takeaway...

Nathan gave Tony a heads up about the theme of the lesson and the type of ALT he was hoping to use. When they got together later that week, Tony did not disappoint. He brought along his wood chopper's wedge and a marker. Nathan couldn't wait to hear how Tony planned to integrate these into the lesson. Tony laid it out. "When you mentioned you were hoping to involve a couple of the boys more, I started considering how we might connect them with the theme of division. It occurred to me that many folks in our community split their own firewood, so they would know what a wedge is used for. After I looked at the passage, I thought we could challenge our group to each handle the wedge and write on it ideas that divide. On one side, things that divided the first century church in Corinth. On the other side, things that divide Christians today. As each kid handles the two-pound wedge, he gets a feel for the weight of his own behavior in causing hurtful divisions." Wow! Nathan was astounded by the creativeness of this teen. The idea touched all the bases—a chance to connect with a familiar tool, the feel of a symbol of the main idea, a challenge to express their understanding of the lesson concepts, and a unique way to communicate what they had learned. This was going to be exciting!

Teacher Reflection:

1. The Mindset of Teachers Who Embrace Differentiation:

Gregory and Chapman discuss these perspectives that are both inspiring and challenging. Rate yourself on a scale of 1-5 with 5 being "strongly agree" and 1 being "strongly disagree" as you consider each statement:

- Each teen has special strengths.
- Each teen has areas that need improvement.
- God has made each teen unique.
- Learning takes place throughout our lives.
- At the beginning of each study, teens bring their own perspective and prior learning.
- How a teen feels influences his/her learning.
- All teens can change and grow.
- Teens grasp new concepts in different ways and at different times.[14]

2. Differentiated approach to practicing sharing your faith:

Ask your group members to select from the following list of options related to sharing their faith in Christ. Have them think through how they would approach the situation. Then challenge each one to communicate his/her plan in some way:

- Post on some form of social media.
- Share during a phone call.
- Witness one-on-one in a personal conversation.
- Develop a creative way to communicate Christ's love with an act of service.
- Write a one verse tract including an attractive layout.

- I will share my plan with the group leader, with a close friend, in a small group, or in front of the entire group.

---

[1] Gayle H. Gregory and Carolyn Chapman, *Differentiated Instructional Strategies: One Size Doesn't Fit All*, 3rd ed. (Thousand Oaks: Corwin, 2013), 3.

[2] Earl, Lorna. *Assessment As Learning: Using Classroom Assessment to Maximize Student Learning*. (Thousand Oaks: Corwin Press, 2003.) Quoted in Carol Ann Tomlinson and Marcia B. Imbeau, *Leading and Managing a Differentiated Classroom* (Alexandria: ASCD, 2010), 27.

[3] Carol Ann Tomlinson, *How to Differentiate Instruction in Mixed-Ability Classrooms* (Alexandria: ASCD, 2001), 1.

[4] Tomlinson, *Leading and Managing*, 31.

[5] Peter T. O'Brien, *Colossians, Philemon*, World Biblical Commentary, eds. David A. Hubbard et al. (Waco: Word Books, 1982), 88.

[6] Tomlinson, *Leading and Managing*, 34.

[7] O'Brien, *Colossians, Philemon*, 90.

[8] N. T. Wright, *The Epistles of Paul to The Colossians and to Philemon: An Introduction and Commentary*, Tyndale New Testament Commentaries, ed. Canon Leon Morris (Grand Rapids: William B. Eerdmans Publishing Company, 1986), 93.

[9] O'Brien, *Colossians, Philemon*, 88.

[10] Wright, *The Epistles of Paul*, 97-98.

[11] Tomlinson, *Leading and Managing*, 19.

[12] Judy Willis, *Research-Based Strategies to Ignite Student Learning: Insights From a Neurologist and Classroom Teacher* (Alexandria: ASCD, 2006), 4.

[13] Roger W. Mackey, "Strategies That Promote Greater Student Engagement and Professor Enjoyment" The Teaching Professor Annual Conference Educate...Engage...Inspire (lecture, Renaissance Washington, Washington, DC, June 3, 2016).

[14] Gregory and Chapman, *Differentiated Instructional Strategies*, 2-3.

HOW DID THE TEACHER MASTER THE MATERIAL?

Effective teachers are aware of their own thinking and model this for their teens.

Nathan was stumped. He had read the passage three times, but he was still bewildered. In his passion for leading his students to deepen their faith in Christ, Nathan chose Hebrews two as the focal passage for that week. As he unpacked verse 17, he read, "He (Jesus) had to be like His brothers in every way, so that He could become a merciful and faithful high priest in service to God, to make propitiation for..." (HCSB). Wait a second, Nathan thought. I am lost. But this is so important and I have to get this right. Then the idea struck him—as I explore this passage, I am going to record my thinking process and share with my group how I work through the passage!

Nathan is really focused on a valuable approach to teaching...sharing with your students how you went about learning a particular skill or some new content. Perhaps you have met the extraordinary leader or athlete or musician to whom you pose the question, "How did you figure this out?" Or put another way, "What are you thinking about as you perform?" Perhaps the expert provides you with an insightful description of what he is thinking. On the other hand, perhaps his response to your question is met with a blank stare or a shrug and the comment, "I don't know. It's instinct."

Well, this second answer, while sincere, is completely unhelpful for someone hoping to follow in the footsteps of an idol. No one can mentor a disciple without coaching the follower on his mental processes. This chapter is about two related concepts: *metacognition* and *reflective practice*—two practices that educational literature states are instrumental in making teachers more effective.

KEY #5: TRANSFORMATIONAL TEACHERS ARE AWARE OF THEIR OWN THINKING AND MODEL THIS PROCESS FOR THEIR STUDENTS.

Definition: "Thinking about one's thinking with the goal of enhancing learning. In its simplest terms, metacognition involves being mindful of one's thinking processes, such as strategies to puzzle out the meaning of an unfamiliar word or improve recall of specific facts. The goal of teaching students to be metacognitive is to guide them to consciously recognize when and how to employ the thinking and problem-solving strategies that work best for them."[1]

Researchers advocate for teaching students to be aware of their thinking and to take charge of their learning by applying cognitive strategies. Such steps include self-monitoring and self-teaching.

> A crucial finding in the research about metacognition and executive function is that the skills and strategies that permit students to take charge of their learning can be taught. Through explicit instruction, modeling, and encouragement, students can learn to identify and overcome deficiencies in comprehension, reasoning, problem solving, and communication.[2]

As you get your group members accustomed to hearing you describe your thinking processes and strategies, challenge them to reflect on their own metacognitive activity. Encourage them to share with each other, "Here's how I learned this..." Once again, research says that students who learn to consider their learning strategies have significant increase in their learning. Wilson and Conyers state,

"Decades of research analyzing hundreds of classroom research studies offer support for explicit instruction on metacognition and cognition strategies as one of the most effective ways to improve school performance and to help students to achieve their academic potential. Arguably, **guiding students to become metacognitive may be one of the most important aspects of schooling** if we are engaged in schooling that supports those aims."[3] (emphasis added)

This author would like the reader to consider this question—"Have you paused in your lesson preparation to consider how you went about learning the concepts you are preparing to teach?" Taking the time to consider your mental processing is known as *metacognitive analysis*. "*Metacognition* is, put simply, thinking about one's thinking. More precisely, it refers to the processes used to plan, monitor, and assess one's understanding and performance. Metacognition includes a critical awareness of a) one's thinking and learning and b) oneself as a thinker and learner."[4]

Ruth Schoenbach and coauthors give an excellent description of metacognitive conversation in their text, *Reading for Understanding: A Guide to Improving Reading in Middle and High School Classrooms*. The authors explain it this way:

The metacognitive conversation is carried on both internally, as teacher and students individually read and consider their own mental processes, and externally, as they talk about their reading processes, strategies, knowledge resources, and motivations and their interactions with and affective responses to tests.... In metacognitive conversation, then, participants become consciously aware of their mental activity and are able to describe it and discuss it with others. Such conversation enables teachers to make their invisible cognitive activity visible and enables teachers and students to reflectively analyze and assess the impact of their thinking processes. A great deal of research in the past two decades has identified metacognition as key to deep learning and flexible use of knowledge and skills.[5]

For effective instruction, it is not enough to plan and organize opportunities for these types of reflections; it is incumbent upon master teachers to be able to anticipate how students should best approach new information and plan how to assist them with overcoming potential hurdles. Ken Bain and his research team reveal that highly regarded professors have a strong grasp of their discipline and the complex issues that create controversy or uncertainty. Understanding these perplexities help teachers unlock difficult concepts for their students. Bain argues that this ability to think about their own thinking provides them with understanding about how other people might learn. Effective teachers have awareness about what needs to be taught first and can anticipate where their learners may be tripped up. Because of these insights, they can simplify and clarify difficult passages.[6]

Let's practice... The consideration or reflection about one's thinking processes is *metacognition*. The examples below include the actual *metacognitive strategy* a learner chooses to use.

What do you do when you hear a new phone number for the first time?
Possible responses:
- I create a song using the numbers.
- I see a team picture with the numbers on the team jerseys.
- I type out the number on an imaginary keypad on my leg.
- I see the geometric pattern of the numbers on a keypad in my mind.

What do you do when you discover you are "lost" while you are reading?
Possible responses:
- I go back to the last sentence/paragraph where I understood.
- I start over...re-reading the entire chapter or article.
- I jump ahead to a new section and come back later to re-read that section.

What do you do when you begin to prepare a Bible study and you have no idea what the passage is talking about the first time you read it? (Here's where we left off with Nathan...)

Possible responses:

- I re-read the passage numerous times.
- I re-read the passage in different translations.
- I look up unfamiliar terms in a Bible dictionary.
- I go immediately to a trusted commentary for interpretation.

Are you training independent, self-directed disciples?

Jesus instructs in Luke 6:40 that when the disciple is fully trained, he will be like his teacher. Have you thought about assisting your teens in the process of becoming a fully trained, independent disciple? Here's a strong challenge I encountered while writing this chapter:

To become self-directed learners, students must learn to assess the demands of the task, evaluate their own knowledge and skills, plan their approach, monitor their progress, and adjust their strategies as needed.[7]

Can you picture members of your group leading a Bible study at school or in their communities? Where are they going to obtain the skills for such an endeavor? Of course, observing you as you teach and model effective teaching strategies will have a large impact on who they become as teachers. But this chapter's emphasis on meta-cognition points out the value of coaching them on becoming aware of their own thinking processes and strategies. Here are some ways to respond to the challenge stated above. Begin with brief explanations of your personal approach to studying Scripture and preparing a lesson. Next, challenge your teens to talk about their own thinking—for example, what do you find confusing? What is counter to your own thinking in the passage? How do you approach problem solving when you struggle with the meaning of the passage? Third, coach them on self-assessments as they study a passage and construct a lesson. Fourth, offer your teens the opportunity to construct an outline of a passage or a lesson plan, and you watch them teach it. With their approval, video the presentation and allow them to evaluate it and make suggestions for improvement. The focus here is not the finished product, but the higher order problem solving and thinking strategies that went into the product they produced.

You can begin by describing your own thinking progression for something that applies directly to a lesson you are presenting. One group of educators encourage teachers to "think out loud" as you describe how you approach the task and lay out your strategies. Include a reflection on your own strengths and weaknesses. Also, include how you assess your progress—what questions do you ask yourself? And finally, how you evaluate the final product.[8]

I would encourage you to provide scaffolding for these tough concepts for your group members. Think of a construction site where a multi-story building is under construction. Everyone has seen elaborate layers of scaffolding going up around the exterior of the building. And we have all noticed that the scaffolding all disappears as the exterior wall is constructed...the framework is no longer needed. Your students need you to break the various steps into separate pieces and allow them to practice. The next phase involves assisting them with how the pieces fit together. And finally, your disciples are moved from working under your supervision to working autonomously.[9]

William R. Yount, author of *Created to Learn*, describes three different types of metacognition related to our discussion here on the development of independent learners:

Meta-attention: the conscious awareness and regulation of attention. What helps students maintain focus on learning in the group meeting or in personal devotions? For example, students ask themselves, "Do I pay closer attention in the front of the group? Do I focus better while I am studying if I am listening to music?"

Meta-communication: the awareness and regulation of modes of communication—speaking, writing, listening, and reading. Teachers who model good speaking and listening skills help demonstrate these to their students.

Meta-memory: the awareness of strategies that help someone strengthen their memory. Most teens will be at a developmental level at which they recognize that their memory is strengthened if they hear something or if they can see a representation of it.[10]

Rollins outlines three strategies that help teens monitor their own comprehension, summarize key ideas, and stay engaged in and focused on the content. Here are Rollins' three techniques:

VIP (Very Important Point)—as your group members work through a passage, they can use a highlighter to indicate a VIP phrase or verse. After completing the passage, they can go back and explain why they highlighted the portions they chose.

Sticky notes—as individuals study a passage, they jot down reactions, questions, or summary statements on sticky notes. The restricted space requires that students think more carefully about how they express their thoughts.

Coding—this strategy works well when the passage has two or three main ideas for which the teacher and/or teens can create a code that can be written in the margin. For a first time reading of Matthew 5:13-16 a reader could mark blocks of verses with **J/G** standing for *Jesus/Grace*. By contrast, other sections can be marked **P/L** for *Pharisees/Legalism*. Another coding exercise could be reading the four chapters of Jonah and mark each section with **BA** for *bad attitude*, or **SA** for *selfish attitude*, or **GA** for *godly attitude*.[11]

Mind, Brain, and Education Research...

Here's a powerful quote that connects the major ideas under discussion:

Metacognition—knowledge about one's own thoughts and the facts that influence one's thinking and learning—can optimize learning. Despite all the information neuroimaging and brain mapping have yielded about the acquisition of information, some of the best strategies are those that students recognize themselves. Research has demonstrated that optimal learners practice distinct behaviors. After a lesson when students are prompted to recognize a breakthrough success in the learning processing that they experienced that day, they should reflect on what they did right...Students benefit from multiple opportunities to practice the metacognitive process of making the unconscious conscious.[12]

I once watched my daughter miss a foul shot in an important high school basketball game. She missed it because her shot lacked the necessary arch. I knew that it was not helpful or necessary for me to call out, "Put more arc on it." I could tell that she was rehearsing in her mind, "Down the chimney..." This was a mental strategy to picture a shot with the correct amount of arc. She swished the next shot to put her team ahead. *Self-reflection. Self-correction. Success.*

Reflective practice...

Reflective practice is that which prevents a teacher from becoming a veteran instructor who has merely repeated the same errors of a first year teacher over and over for thirty years! Stronge describes this practice as follows:

> Effective teachers continually practice self-evaluation and self-critique as learning tools. Reflective teachers portray themselves as students of learning. They are curious about the art and science of teaching and about themselves as effective teachers. They constantly improve lessons, think about how to reach particular children, and seek and try out new approaches in the classroom to better meet the needs of their learners.[13]

Figure 1 depicts the process employed by an educator who is committed to engaging his/her students in ways that lead to the construction of understanding, deep learning, and the continued and confident use of new knowledge. That which leads to transformation!

These are concepts of extreme importance. One would predict that few adults preparing for becoming educational leaders of ministries have ever considered these broad issues while reflecting on their own learning processes. Most certainly they stopped short of interacting with their fellow teachers about their personal experiences. The model in Figure 1 has been developed to describe the relationship between metacognitive analysis and reflective practice with active learning for those preparing to become effective teachers of God's Word.

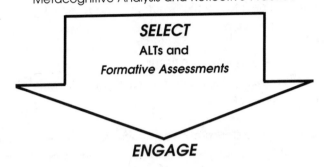

REFLECT
Metacognitive Analysis and Reflective Practice

SELECT
ALTs and
Formative Assessments

ENGAGE

STUDENTS IN LEARNING PROCESS

Figure 1 Teaching and learning process that leads to engagement.[14]
**Coley, "Active Learning Techniques in the
Christian Education Classroom and in Ministry Contexts."**

A Practical Illustration...

Do you have any experience playing/coaching a team sport or singing/directing a choir? Both of these pursuits beautifully illustrate the concept of reflecting on both your performance and the actions and reactions around you. The directors and performers in sports and music are vivid illustrations of an obsession with getting better. Checking statistics. Reading reviews and critiques. Watching video tape of practice and past performances. In the case of many athletic competitions, this is happening during the game! As a coach of dozens of teams over three decades, I can tell you that most mornings around 3:00 AM following a game the previous night, I found myself wide awake—reliving every possession, analyzing every at bat, grieving every missed opportunity to score.

But do we have the same commitment when it comes to our teaching episodes?

While conducting a teachers' training seminar at a church not long ago, I had a participant respond to the concept of *reflective practice* in this testimony:

"Ken, I teach the Bible study lesson three times every week:
The first time, I go through it mid-week after I finish studying.
The second time, I teach the lesson on Sunday morning.
The third time, I teach it again in the car on my way home after church.
THE THIRD TIME IS ALWAYS THE BEST!"
And I responded, "This process means you will be a better teacher every week."

Reflective practice stands between your improving every year and you being a first year teacher over and over for thirty years. So what are you evaluating in regard to your teaching? Here are just a few of the dimensions of teaching for reflection:

Was the content presented in ways that allowed for *construction of understanding*? (Ch. 1)
Did the presentation and activities connect with the *schema* of my audience? (Ch. 2)
Was everyone *engaged* in the ALTs? Did they work? Any holdouts? (Ch. 3)
Did I approach the group in ways that acknowledged *differences*? (Ch. 4)
Did I model or describe *how I went about learning* this material? (Ch. 5)
Did I include opportunities for them to *work together* on a task? (Ch. 6)
Did I weave in *formative assessments* to check for understanding? (Ch. 7)
Did my *lesson plan flow smoothly* with an emphasis on God's Word? (Ch. 8)

As you progress in your teaching experience, you will have these concepts so ingrained in your mind, you will find yourself making adjustments in your lesson plan and activities while you teach! If you sense a drop in energy level in the group during your lesson, you can, with experience, introduce another method to magnify God's Word in ways that are effective and meaningful.

The Power of How I Learned This...

I am a visual learner "off the chart." I find I must convert any important information I hear to some type of visual representation—letters, numbers, pictures, diagrams. While studying for a major exam, I decided to convert all the information I needed to remember into one large portrait. Each object in my imaginary room was a reminder of one point on my outline. Thankfully, I was able to recall the information and do well on the exam. Since then I have coached others on how to organize large amounts of material in ways that are personally meaningful. Twenty-five years later I can still reproduce the picture.

Hall and Simeral have some challenging ideas for the teacher who really wants to improve and is willing to spend time reflecting. They suggest getting a journal and writing entries for each lesson that include a WOW! (something that was a success) and a Yikes! (something that surprised you or a technique that didn't work). Second, using a list of all your group members, jot down one or more interests each one has. For any marked Not Sure, make a point to get to know those kids. Third, recruit a fellow teacher with whom you can be transparent and exchange ideas related to various aspects of lesson preparation and pedagogy.[15]

)))

Nathan's takeaway...

Nathan began the study that week by reading the focal passage out loud—Hebrews 2:14-18, asking his group to listen for unfamiliar terms and ideas. After he finished reading the five verses aloud, he listed on chart paper all the points of confusion the teens mentioned, including the term *propitiation*. His next step was to explain in some detail how he had been stumped by a couple of the verses earlier in the week. He held up his Bible in which he had used red, yellow, and green highlighters as he made note of sections he understood and sections he needed to work on. He also showed them the Post-It® Notes attached to the margins on which he had written questions like, What does "He did not reach out to help angels" mean? As the Bible study continued, Nathan distributed brief portions of commentaries and Bible dictionaries he had used and challenged his teens to join in the investigation, rather than merely spoon feed them the results of his research. Throughout the study, he encouraged them to articulate their own thought patterns and strategies. The end result was a deeper understanding of the passage itself and the experience of using techniques a student of the Bible can use in his own study.

《《《

Teacher Reflection:

1. Do you recall the step-by-step process that a parent, teacher, or coach used to help you with a new skill? For example, learning to hit a baseball or golf ball, a new song on a musical instrument, or a new recipe in the kitchen. Are you able to retrieve these strategies from your memory and use them with your own teens? Now, consider how you might do the same with Bible study techniques that you use every week as you prepare the lesson.

2. Select an unfamiliar Bible passage and use the three strategies described in this chapter: VIP, sticky notes, and coding. As you work through the passage, reflect on your metacognitive processes and consider how you can explain these to the teens in your group.

---

[1] Donna Wilson and Marcus Conyers, *Five Big Ideas for Effective Teaching: Connecting Mind, Brain, and Education Research to Classroom Practice* (New York: Teachers College Press, 2013), 110.

[2] Ibid., 117.

[3] Ibid., 110.

[4] Nancy Chick, "Metacognition," Vanderbilt University Center for Teaching, (accessed May 20, 2014), http://cft.vanderbilt.edu/guides-sub-pages/metacognition/.

[5] Ruth Schoenback, Cynthia Greenleaf, Lynn Murphy, *Reading for Understanding: A Guide to Improving Reading in Middle and High School Classrooms*, Jossey-Bass Education Series (Hoboken: Wiley, 1999), 25.

[6] Ken Bain, *What the Best College Teachers Do* (Cambridge: Harvard University Press, 2004), 25.

[7] Susan A. Ambrose et al., *How Learning Works: Seven Research-Based Principles for Smart Teaching* (San Francisco: Jossey-Bass, 2010), 191.

[8] Ibid., 192-211.

[9] Ibid., 214-215.

[10] William R. Yount, *Created to Learn: A Christian Teacher's Introduction to Educational Psychology*, 2nd ed. (Nashville, TN): B&H Academic, 2010), 297-298.

[11] Suzy Pepper Rollins, *Learning in the Fast Lane: Eight Ways to Put All Students on the Road to Academic Success* (Alexandria, VA.: ASCD, 2014), 100-103.

[12] Judy Willis, *Research-Based Strategies to Ignite Student Learning: Insights From a Neurologist and Classroom Teacher* (Alexandria: ASCD, 2006), 32-33.

[13] James H. Stronge, *Qualities of Effective Teachers*, 2nd ed. (Alexandria: ASCD, 2007), 30.

[14] Kenneth S. Coley, "Active Learning Techniques in the Christian Education Classroom and in Ministry Contexts," *Christian Education Journal* 9, no. 2 (Fall 2012): 362.

[15] Pete Hall and Alisa Simeral, *Teach Reflect Learn: Building Your Capacity for Success in the Classroom* (Alexandria: ASCD, 2015), 56-60.

Chapter 6

WHY DO SO MANY TEENS DISLIKE GROUP WORK?

Effective teachers skillfully design cooperative learning activities so the results are positive and productive.

Nathan wanted to shake things up. While the Bible studies were going well, he noticed that the group members tended to sit in the same spots and talk to the same buddies each week. He wanted more for his group's interaction with each other than being accepting and polite. Reflecting on his past experiences in athletics, he recalled that the most memorable practices and games included teamwork under pressure. Somehow it always brought out the best in teammates and everyone got better. Could the same chemistry exist in his group? What could he do to bring this about?

For some readers and teachers, the next key to transformational teaching is a tough sell—*cooperative learning* (a.k.a. *group work*). So let's start with the negative background noise that accompanies this instructional technique. Pause for a moment and consider your own preferences and previous experiences. Often the criticism focuses on the assignment—perhaps vague, undoable in a reasonable timeframe, or too easy or too difficult for the group. Sometimes the disapproval revolves around the group process—some folks watch while those considered to be stronger students do all the work. Or maybe the knot in your stomach is a result of the product that the group produced—somehow missing the point, not authentically connected to the main point of the lesson, or worst of all, no one even asked to see your response or work product. From a leader's perspective this teaching method could possibly become a waste of valuable class time.

Stay with me, please. It just doesn't have to be this way. Without getting into technical educational research, I want to point out that educators have proves this approach to learning is highly effective. Researches have seen successful outcomes when cooperative learning is properly implemented. "Using cooperative learning helps teachers lay the foundation for student success in a world that depends on collaboration and cooperation."[1]

Looking at this another way, think how often in your professional life, your church ministry experience, and your family life do you work independently and in isolation. Most adults respond that in all of these settings they depend on colleagues or partners or a spouse to reason through problem solving and decision making. And in many settings (hopefully our local congregations), these skills are invaluable for reaching significant decisions and effectively implementing agreed upon strategies. And where do our church members learn these attitudes and skills?

> **KEY #6: COOPERATIVE LEARNING INVOLVES GROUP PARTICIPANTS WORKING TOGETHER IN SMALL GROUPS TO ACCOMPLISH A SPECIFIC TASK SUCH AS ANALYZING A PASSAGE, EXPLORING SOLUTIONS TO A PROBLEM, OR CREATING NEW WAYS OF DOING MINISTRY.**

This ALT is also known as "collaborative learning."[2]

We began this chapter with a candid review of some of the popular criticism of this approach to teaching. However, a host of studies have produced a frequently cited list of factors that researchers say will lead to productive cooperative learning experiences for you and your Bible study group. The five factors are described below:

Elements of Cooperative Learning by Johnson & Johnson® (1975)

Positive Interdependence: The group's success depends on everyone's cooperation. Each participant is assigned a role to play in the group's process.

Face-to-Face Promotive Interaction: A spirit of respect, encouragement, and support for each group member pervades the group process.

Individual and Group Accountability: Each member is expected to contribute and the group is expected to present the results or work product to the larger group.

Interpersonal and Small Group Skills: Communication skills and conflict resolution techniques are discussed so trust is built.

Group Processing: Time is allotted to reflect on the group's interaction.[3]

Provide a Meaningful Task: The goal or work product needs to connect with the group members so they view their efforts to be relevant and the work product authentic. (This element was added by Frey, Fisher, & Everlove (2009)).[4]

One of the most vivid illustrations of these elements of cooperative learning can be found in the book of Nehemiah. In this narrative Nehemiah, the new construction foreman, has a Herculean task before him—the restoration of the wall of Jerusalem. The previous structure was a protective fortress that encircled the city, but decades after Babylonians attack God's holy city, the wall was a 2.5-mile pile of rubble. Chapter two concludes with Nehemiah calling the citizens of Jerusalem together to give themselves to *a meaningful task.* Chapter three describes how Nehemiah divided the workers in subgroups and assigned the work by communities. Families were assigned to restore the particular gate and portion of the wall that stood next to their neighborhood. *Positive interdependence* is on display as we read how each section of the wall was restored beginning at the Sheep Gate (3:1) and moving counter-clockwise around the layout of the structure. *Face-to-face promotive interaction* permeated the teamwork necessary for Nehemiah's followers to serve both as construction workers and security monitors. This double duty is described in 4:15-23. This passage further illustrates *individual and group accountability*, in that "half of my men did the work while the other half held spears, shields, bows and armor." Nehemiah five describes the exceptional leadership skills that Nehemiah employed while a large portion of the construction force worked through a major conflict involving taxes, mortgages, and usury (5:1-19). Following the completion of the wall, Nehemiah and Ezra led the citizens of Jerusalem in a worship experience that included but far exceeded *group processing*—"then they worshiped the Lord with their faces to the ground" (8:6).

As you get started with making use of cooperative learning, here are some recommendations that will make your early attempts more successful.

Tips for Improving the Performance of Your Groups[5]

1. *Organize your groups to include a variety of ability levels.* Experts have found that weaker students actually perform worse when they are placed in a group with other low performing students. So avoid homogenous groups.
2. *Cooperative learning groups should be kept small*—three to four group members. Remember element #1? Each participant needs to play a role in the process, such as discussion leader, note taker, timer, presenter, etc.
3. *Cooperative learning should be used consistently but not over-used.* Not every lesson is going to lend itself to this approach.

Mind, Brain, and Education Research...

One neuroscientist explains, "When students build their working memories through a variety of activities, they are stimulating multiple sensory intake centers in their brains. Their brains develop pathways leading to the same memory storage destination. By stimulating several senses with the information, more brain connections are available when students need to recall that memory later on.[6]

Think of assisting your group members to recall and access information as one makes use of a storage unit that you rent near your home.

You take belongings there for safe keeping and easy retrieval. The more avenues and side streets there are to get to and from the storage unit, the better! Some of the findings are based on MRI experiments. "Some of the strategies suggested by neuroimaging are ones that have students personalize information to be learned, thereby further activating the areas of the brain that help form memories."[7] Cooperative learning is a method that powerfully delivers these connections.

Scaffolding skill development—my kids aren't ready to do this!

Most teens will need some coaching and practice, particularly if they come from a competitive school environment in which students strive to finish first and score independently. It would be too ambitious for most groups to start with one of the lengthy cooperative learning activities described at the end of this chapter. Beginning in small increments such as the *Think-Pair-Share* ALT prepares group members to make a contribution, listen attentively to another teen, and then articulate the results to the entire group. The next step can be *Think-Pair-Square-Share*: the previous activity but with the additional step of two pairs presenting to each other before sharing with the entire group. Again, communication, listening, prioritizing, and summarizing skills are being developed. A third step in the ramping up of teamwork skills could be a brief assignment given to small groups of 3-4 to discuss a passage of Scripture and resolve a problem or reach a conclusion. This assignment would include a tight timeframe of 3-4 minutes, no more. Pressure usually inspires focus and productivity.

From the Gospels...

Jesus demonstrated patient skill development as he carried out His three-year ministry and trained His disciples to carry on after His ascension. He provided time to talk among themselves (Matt. 16:13), He gave them small tasks under His supervision (Matt 14:15-21), and He sent them out in pairs to witness (Mark 6:7-13). Frey, Fisher, and Everlove describe this process as "the gradual release of responsibility model" of teaching.[8] Figure A depicts the moving of responsibility for performing a task from the teacher to the students. Considering their approach, particularly in light of the Gospel illustrations cited above, helps us identify when and how a cooperative learning activity best fits into a typical lesson. Figure A depicts how the leader introduces the lesson focus (level 1), guides students through the initial stages of investigation (level 2), the students participate in collaborative learning (level 3), and each group member is challenged to apply the information independently (level 4).[9]

Figure A: The Gradual Release of Responsibility Model by Frey, Fisher, and Everlove[10]

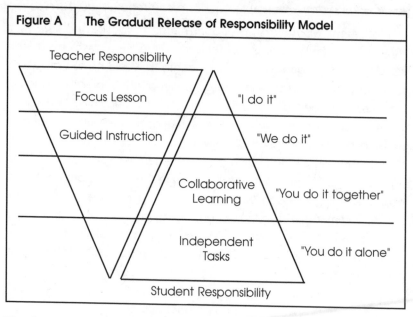

| Figure A | The Gradual Release of Responsibility Model |

Teacher Responsibility

Focus Lesson — "I do it"

Guided Instruction — "We do it"

Collaborative Learning — "You do it together"

Independent Tasks — "You do it alone"

Student Responsibility

The Power of a Group to Create

I have had the blessing to present in international settings such as: Haiti, Cuba, and the Congo (DRC). In each of these settings, as well as those across the US, I included the opportunity for participants to work in a small group (3-4) with the expectation that they would create something. Each time, without fail, something magical happened. These assignments always provided the team with the potential to design something brand new. And the never-seen-before result usually has the finger prints of all the team members. The end result often results in cell phone pictures that record their workmanship for future reference.

More challenging cooperative learning activities:

In his book, *The Classes They Remember*, David Sherrin outlines three types of role plays:

1) The Full Class Role Play: An example of Scripture that would lend itself to involving your entire group as a whole would include the conquest of Jericho in Joshua 6, the feeding of the 5,000 in Matthew 14, or the day of Pentecost in Acts 2. The benefit of this activity is that everyone is involved and performing in unison. Luke 8:40, a street scene involving a large, smothering crowd would be another potentially powerful passage that could involve a number of participants.

2) The Fish Bowl: In this option only a small portion of the entire group is performing, but all group members can still be involved. For example, five group members could each take the role of Job, his wife, or one of the three friends—Elizphaz, Bildad, and Zophar. The five would perform pre-arranged dialogues, and the remainder of the group would sit in a circle around the characters. The observers would interact with the characters at prescribed times or at the conclusion of a scene by asking questions like, "Why does the character respond to Job in such a cold or distant way?" A New Testament passage that would lend itself to this option would be any dialogue Jesus had with a small group of people or an event like the Mount of Transfiguration in Luke 9.

3) Small Group Role-Plays: This third option would be ideal for working through a passage that has the potential to be understood or performed in different ways. For example, Luke 6:6-11 describes the healing of a man with a paralyzed hand on a Sabbath. The miracle is observed by scribes and Pharisees, who begin plotting against Jesus as the scene closes. Another application might be dramatizing the three parables involving the lost coin, the lost sheep, and the lost son, with each group being assigned its own parable.

4) Debates: Many passages of Scripture involve pivotal decisions that altered the course of history. Re-enact the report of the spies that checked out the Promised Land. Or call together The Jerusalem Council (Acts 15) and have Peter, James, and Paul present their arguments.

Sherrin advises that "For an historical role-play, we need an event that has a gripping story, historical importance, abundant conflict, and a large cast of characters who are involved in most events."

He provides the following outline to assist teachers in coaching their groups and guiding their preparation:

Questions to establish background, context, and conflict:

- What do we need to know about the story? What is the situation?
- What do we need to know about the characters and their relationships?
- What is the conflict? What are the stakes of this conflict?[12]

Going to another level...

In his second book, *Judging for Themselves*, Sherrin describes the power of setting up mock trials. Here's his argument:

> Here is why I do mock trials: they are challenging, authentic projects in which students create and then do something "real." The projects serve as both learning and assessment tools since students learn from doing the work and teachers have a tangible product for evaluating understanding and growth. Mock trials are engaging for students and the role-playing aspect gets them out of their chairs, collaborating, and entering into the mindsets and perspectives of their characters.[13]

The account of several trials are included in Scripture and would provide outstanding material for a challenging group project. Here are some examples:

- The arrest and prosecution of Jesus
- The arrest and trial of Peter and John in Acts 4
- The arrest and interrogation of the disciples before the Sanhedrin in Acts 5
- The accusation, trial, and stoning of Stephen in Acts 6 and 7
- The plot against Paul and his defense before Felix in Acts 23-27

Crafting this activity can involve some or all of these steps: selecting and teaching the passage of Scripture, selecting a defendant, choosing witnesses, deciding where to hold the mock trial, creating exhibits and other forms of evidence, and assigning group members to different roles.[14]

Connecting the Dots...

When teachers skillfully craft cooperative learning activities that enhance their lesson delivery, they are teaching in a way that demonstrate the first five keys:

Key #1: Cooperative learning results in opportunities for the *construction of understanding* as ideas are articulated, insights are exchanged, and creative projects are produced.

Key #2: Cooperative learning involves group members' *prior learning and experiences,* which should be reflected in the results of the team's efforts.

Key #3: Cooperative learning is best done in small teams so all participants are *engaged* in the endeavor and contribute in meaningful ways to the results.

Key #4: Cooperative learning allows for a *diversity* of assignments (look at this passage or discuss this issue), of process within the team (reading, interpreting, notetaking, structuring ideas, etc.), and of work products (verbal response, dramatic presentation, visual representation, etc.)

Key #5: Cooperative learning can be structured in ways that challenge individuals to reflect on their own *metacognitive processing* related to the assigned task..."when I examine a difficult passage, I like to begin by..."

》》

Nathan's takeaway...

After reviewing all his new teaching tools, Nathan decided to use "Fish Bowl" for his upcoming lesson on Genesis 3: The Fall of Man. He recruited three students whom he believed ready for the task of preparing and presenting in this setting. Nathan chose the role of the Creator to be his part and allowed the three teens to select from the remaining three characters: Adam, Eve, and Satan. Each participant was to study the passage, focusing on his part. Three nights before their group meeting, the four got together and prepared a script. At the Bible study, attendees chose a seat near one of the characters, not knowing which role he or she was performing. Twice during the dialogue Nathan stopped the presentation to allow for questioning of the actors by the audience seated near them. The audience participated by asking questions like, "When you heard the decision Eve made, what made you most angry? What was your greatest fear?" As Nathan reflected on the evening, he was convinced some deep learning and upper level thinking had taken place.

Teacher Reflection:

1. What hurdles do you think you face when you consider asking your teens to work together in a group? Which "smaller" ALTs might help prepare them to take on a larger task in a larger team?

2. As you consider your ministry with your teens, what larger purposes might benefit from your students learning to work together effectively in a small group? For example, do you attempt ministry teams for the purpose of planning, ministering through service groups, or presenting the Gospel in small groups? Think through the interpersonal skills needed that might be developed through cooperative learning experiences.

---

[1] Ceri B. Dean et al., *Classroom Instruction That Works: Research-Based Strategies for Increasing Student Achievement*, 2nd ed. (Alexandria: ASCD, 2012), 35.

[2] Nancy Frey, Douglas Fisher, and Sandi Everlove, *Productive Group Work: How to Engage Students, Build Teamwork, and Promote Understanding* (Alexandria: ASCD, 2009), 4.

[3] David W. Johnson and Roger T. Johnson, *Learning Together and Alone: Cooperative, Competitive, and Individualistic Learning* (Englewood Cliffs: Prentice-Hall, 1975).

[4] Frey, Fisher, and Everlove, *Productive Group Work*, 20.

[5] Robert J. Marzano, Debra J. Pickering, and Jane E. Pollock, *Classroom Instruction That Works: Research-Based Strategies for Increasing Student Achievement* (Alexandria: ASCD, 2001), 87-88.

[6] Judy Willis, *Research-Based Strategies to Ignite Student Learning: Insights From a Neurologist and Classroom Teacher* (Alexandria: ASCD, 2006), 10.

[7] Ibid.

[8] Frey, Fisher, and Everlove, *Productive Group Work*, 6.

[9] Ibid., 6-7.

[10] Ibid., 7.

[11] David Sherrin, *The Classes They Remember: Using Role-Plays to Bring Social Studies and English to Life* (New York: Routledge, 2016), 12.

[12] Ibid. 28.

[13] David Sherrin, *Judging for Themselves: Using Mock Trials to Bring Social Studies and English to Life* (New York: Routledge, 2016), xiv.

[14] Sherrin, *Judging for Themselves*, 4.

Chapter 7

WE ARE HAVING FUN, BUT HOW DO I KNOW THE TEENAGERS ARE LEARNING ANYTHING?

Effective teachers include brief assessments that provide evidence of student learning.

Nathan's Bible studies were really going well—attendance was up, the group atmosphere was very positive, and the teens were consistently engaged. Each week he would do his usual de-brief and reflect on how the participants responded to the Active Learning Techniques he had planned. But at the corner of his mind was a nagging question...were they really learning and retaining anything? Did high energy and enthusiastic participation translate to transformation? Nathan was not sure how to tackle this next step.

I am confident you could fund your next mission trip if you had a nickel for each time you heard this statement: the trouble with the church is that it is an inch deep and a mile wide! There are many facets to this truism. One dimension may be we as biblical teachers and leaders seldom park the bus and take time to assess where our learners are. Are individuals properly processing Scripture each week? Can they accurately express biblical concepts in their own words? Are attitudes and behaviors being transformed?

As soon as I suggest interrupting the flow of a lesson to "park the bus" and evaluate students' comprehension, some teachers are worried that the flow will be lost, valuable time will be wasted, and let's don't forget the #1 objection: "I won't be able to get through all my notes!"

Please stick with me as we think through brief, creative ways to evaluate your students' grasp of the new concepts you are presenting.

As we have done in each chapter, let's take a look at the teaching techniques of the Master Teacher. The Gospels have many examples of Jesus asking questions to a variety of audiences:

Matthew 22:42—"*What do you think about the Christ, whose son is He?*"

Mark 8:27—"*Who do people say that I am?*"

Luke 18:41—"*What do you want Me to do for you?*"

John 18:34—"*Are you saying this on your own initiative, or did others tell you about Me?*"

Just to clarify, at no time did Jesus ask a question because He needed information. But He did use questions to direct people's thinking and force them to evaluate their prior perspective or understanding. You and I need to hear from our group members or observe their facial reactions to collect data about their comprehension. Clearly Jesus did not. But He used questions as a way to challenge His listeners to collect their thoughts and communicate their level of understanding. This is called *formative assessment* by educators today.

KEY #7: EFFECTIVE TEACHERS INCLUDE BRIEF ASSESSMENTS THAT PROVIDE EVIDENCE OF STUDENT LEARNING.

Definition: *Formative assessments* are brief evaluations that take place during group meeting time and provide valuable feedback to both the leader and the participants.

The aspect that makes this unlike a final exam is that the assessment takes place while the instruction is ongoing and both teacher and student can adjust their approach while the lesson and concepts are being formed, not later when the best opportunity for learning has passed.[1]

Jesus met the needs of His learners in the teaching/learning process.

Jesus magnificently demonstrates these concepts in Luke 9:18 (and following verses) when He inquires of His disciples, "Who do the crowds say I am?" (NIV, 1984 version). Being aware that His disciples were dealing with major-league cognitive dissonance, Jesus wanted them to express what they were hearing from others, as even His closest followers attempted to sort out His identity. Their responses were all over the map: "Some say John the Baptist; others say Elijah; and still others, that one of the prophets of long ago has come back to life" (v. 19, NIV). He was acutely aware that their prior religious training had established a strongly held perspective that made it extremely problematic to make sense of His ministry and miracles. His followers were cataloguing scattered pieces of information and experiences, but they weren't getting it. Jesus knew if they had a quiz on any given day, most of them would fail. But instead of bullying ahead with more lecture material, the Savior of the world demonstrated for us how to meet the needs of our learners.

Stop and have a formative assessment right now before reading the next few pages. Consider this teaching episode from Luke 9 and see how many of the previously discussed Keys from chapters 1-6 you can identify in this brief instructional dialogue. No rush...we'll wait.

1. The disciples needed a change in understanding...He had to begin with their schema.

As the Master Teacher, Jesus was aware that all learners bring to new learning episodes pre-existing perspectives, dispositions, and attitudes, as well as a knowledge base. To make matters more challenging for Him, as well as for us, this background varies widely from student to student. Researchers and educators call this the learner's *schema*—mental categories that influence a learner's reaction to new ideas. Simplifying brain research on learning, we could say that a student picks up new ideas and asks, "Where do I put this? Do I have an existing file folder for this? If so, which file does this fit with? If not, do I really need this? So where does this fit?"

In the context of this discussion, Jesus certainly was cognizant of the prior training the disciples had received about the nation's hope for a Messiah. Added with that anticipation were snapshots of past prophets, some of whom spoke with authority the way Jesus did and even occasionally were part of a miracle from God...all well-established concepts in the minds of the disciples.

For us, Jesus demonstrated that effective teachers are aware of the schema or background of their students and find ways to connect with or "hook" the lesson to prior learning. We will return to this idea in the final chapter of the book as we lay out a recommended teaching outline for adult Bible study.

2. The disciples needed help with their misconceptions...Teachers prepare by making a metacognitive/thinking analysis of their own learning.

Closely related to the disciples' first need is their need to clarify and correct faulty thinking about His identity. Of course, Jesus didn't need to "figure this out" or "think through a creative approach to get at the misconception," but nonetheless, He demonstrated great teaching for us. Effective teachers spend time thinking through how they learned specific concepts: What was tricky? What was counter to what was expected? What needed to be broken into pieces to add learning and retention? This is referred to as a *metacognitive* analysis, or put simply, "thinking about thinking." Jesus knew the pitfalls and inconsistencies in their thinking, and He certainly had not experienced any difficulty with "misconceptions" Himself. But in this one question He posed to them, He presents for us a model of effective engagement. Chapter three will explore this discussion in more detail.

3. The disciples needed to have a chance to articulate what others were saying...Jesus provided them with a chance to connect their schema with new concepts.

I have done some traveling around our country and have visited quite a few countries outside the United States. It is incredible the misunderstanding and confusion regarding the time period in our history known as the Civil War. Particularly amazing is how "the facts" surrounding the events and causes that led up to this divisive period in our nation's history are presented in classrooms in Virginia in comparison with classrooms in Pennsylvania. An observer to conversations with adults in these two states, which are less than one hundred miles apart, might think he is listening to opinions about events that took place at two entirely different times all together. The variation in the appreciation of what occurred could also be very different.

Can you see how different backgrounds and prior experience can add learning or create major interference? Perhaps your students have a multitude of cultural backgrounds from around the country and the world. How about different religious or denominational backgrounds? Many of us are familiar with the large reservoir of information known as "Sunday School answers," but we have participants in Bible study every week that have no such back log of information. Our missionaries have a real challenge when communicating with non-believers who have prior religious beliefs that are syncretistic, that is worshipers of multiple gods who are open to "adding" another god or deity to their gallery of gods. Such thinking in one's background makes it confusing to consider Jesus Christ, the Way, the Truth, and the Life...there is no other name by which men may be saved.

4. The disciples needed a chance to construct their understanding... Jesus provided them with an active learning experience!

Frequently, Jesus gave His disciples and others the opportunity to voice their understanding of the topic at hand. This necessitates students thinking through their responses, hearing how it sounds as it is stated audibly, and also seeing the reaction of both the teacher and other students. Hopefully, teachers can grasp the value of this process, especially when they compare this to watching and listening passively with no pressure to develop their own thoughts. The remaining chapters of this book will present many Active Learning Techniques that will engage your Bible study participants in learning.

5. The disciples needed some time to work together...He allowed time for cooperative learning.

Social interaction with other learners is a powerful way to engage students. Not only do students get to experience the benefit of expressing their understanding, but they also have the opportunity to hear and learn from other students. There are numerous research findings from educational settings and church-based projects that support the value of discussion, movement, group activities, and cooperative learning. These will be explored in more detail in chapters six, seven, and eight.

Returning to the passage in Luke 9...

Jesus continued the pop quiz, "Who do you say I am?" Only Peter's response is recorded, "The Christ of God" (v. 20). This also illustrates another crucial point: **the role of the Christian educator, as previously stated, is to assist students by stimulating the construction of understanding of absolute Truth within their mental framework and not the manufacturing of a personal, relativistic truth.**

6. **The disciples needed to pause and check their comprehension...Jesus met this need by providing them with a brief time of assessment.**

When was the last time you were in a Bible study and the teacher took a few moments to find out if the class was tracking with him? And asking, "Do you have any questions?" doesn't count. Again, let's be clear, Jesus (unlike you and me) did not need to ask them questions to gage their level of understanding...He knew they didn't get it! But measuring for understanding in brief interactions with your students provides information about levels of comprehension to both the teacher and the student. Perhaps the student was not even aware that he was misunderstanding, as was the case with the disciples. Formative assessment techniques provide both teachers and students with brief snapshots during the lesson. This feedback is extremely useful—the teacher has data to determine whether or not instructional activities need to be adjusted, and students gain insight about their comprehension and can adjust what they are doing.

Mind, Brain, and Education Research...

In most subjects and classes, we tend to teach for a week or two and test on that material only after the extended period of the unit of study. A more brain-attuned method is to assess daily and even several times during a lesson to see what students understand. That is neurological, because if knowledge gaps are not corrected early, the brain will fill in blanks with misinformation. This misinformation may be stored as long-term memories that are difficult to change once embedded.

Sample Formative Assessment Activities

Responding to a Poll:

This is one of the quickest ALTs that includes the nuance of formative assessment. Taking as little as ten seconds, the instructor can gage audience awareness, opinion, or level of understanding. Polling is a popular way of formative assessment. The teacher poses a brief question and asks the class members to respond in one of the following ways:

- Raise your hand if you are familiar with...
- Show me thumbs up or thumbs down if you agree or disagree...
- Show a frequency by the number of fingers you hold up, with your fist being zero.
- Indicate your level of agreement with five being *strongly agree* and so on...
- Select the correct multiple choice answer: one finger is A, two fingers represent B, so on.

Retellings:

This is an excellent choice when the passage involves a narrative sequence. Give participants adequate time to read and think through the sequence of events, summarize the action, and formulate how to express the narrative in their own words. Perhaps you will need to model for your group what this looks like before you assign them their first attempt.[3] A twist on this approach is to ask a small group of participants to summarize a passage in one sentence, attempting to include the 5Ws in the sentence they craft: Who, What, When, Where, and Why.

RAFT:

This formative assessment activity is an acronym and stands for:

Role: What is the role of the writer?
Audience: To whom is the writer writing?
Format: What is the format for the writing?
Topic: What is the focus of the writing?[4]

This is an excellent approach to checking for your group's understanding of the authorship and purpose behind each of the books of the Bible. If some of your older students are ready, you could have them prepare this in advance and present their ideas at the kick off of a new study. Another approach would be to assign them the task of developing a *RAFT* during the mid-point of a study, after you have presented background material over a period of lessons.

Whip Around:

If you need a quick, high energy assessment for the overall understanding of your group, a *whip around* will give you snapshots of their comprehension. First, the teacher asks each member to respond to a short question, such as make a list of three reasons for...in the text. Each student responds on a notecard. Next, all participants stand up. The leader randomly calls on students and each checks off the responses they have on their card that are stated orally. As a student hears his three answers and checks them off, he sits down. As the leader hears the student responses, he has the opportunity to evaluate his groups' level of understanding. Missing from this approach is the opportunity for an assessment of individual's level of comprehension.[5]

Exemplar:

This activity allows students to see an exemplary model for how to carry out a skill. The leader designs a strong example of the concepts presented in the passage. Next, the group is given a list of expectations for measuring the *exemplar*. Third, the *exemplar* is presented and individuals or small groups rate the illustration based on the rubric that was distributed or generated by group discussion.[6] For example, if you are studying Matthew 18:15-17 and discussing how to respond to a believer who sins against you, you could teach through the passage, listing each of the three steps and making note of the themes of restoration and compassion. With this list as your "rubric," you would next present your exemplar and ask the group to identify each of the key concepts. Options for the exemplar could include one the leader writes and distributes as a script and asks members to perform, or a video made in advance of group members performing the script. If the students are unable to identify the separate steps as outlined in the passage, then the leader can be confident that re-teaching is needed.

One-Word Summary:

Ask students to summarize the lesson in one word. Now, have them explain why they selected that word. This would be useful for an email discussion following a teaching session.

One-Minute Paper:

One-Minute Paper or the Half-Sheet Response provides a quick and extremely simple way to collect written feedback on student learning. To use the One-Minute Paper, the teacher stops class two or three minutes early and asks students to respond briefly to some variation on the following two questions. "What was the most important thing you learned during this class?" and "What important questions remain unanswered?"

Muddiest Point:

The technique consists of asking students to jot down a quick response to one question: "What was the muddiest point in ___?" As its name suggest, the Muddiest Point technique provides information on what students find least clear or most confusing about a particular lesson or topic. This can be used as an "exit ticket"—stand at the door and ask for each teen's notecard as he/she exits.

Sit Down:

This assessment technique is often used at the beginning of a session. The leader has everyone stand and begins to fire brief questions rapidly. Participants get to "earn their seats" by responding correctly. (If your group has lots of visitors, allow answers to come from a group or table so the visitors won't be left standing alone. When one member responds correctly, his group sits.)[7]

Pepper (like the baseball drill by the same name):

This assessment technique is fast-paced, high energy. The leader selects 3-4 students who agree to stand and participate in responding to rapid-fire questions. Like the baseball drill, you never know where the ball is going—the participants never know who will field the next question. As students respond, you can continue to hit the same one with questions of ever-increasing difficulty (scaffolding) until he is stumped.

Then toss the same question to another player and keep things moving. Or never ask the same player twice...keep them focused![8]

For example, after a study of one or more of the Gospels, open your study with a review:

Ask player one: Who wrote the first Gospel? Good. Who is his audience? Good. What is another distinction of this book? Great job.

Ask player two: Select another Gospel... Good. How is it similar or different from Matthew? Does it appear that Luke was influenced by other writers?

Ask player three: How is John different from Matthew and Luke? Nice. Can you identify the author? Well done. Was it influenced by the writers of the other Gospels? Great job.

The Power of a Notecard and a Highlighter:

Two items readily available at any office supply company can provide you with significant insight about how your teens individually and collectively are processing new ideas.

Distribute a notecard to each group member and ask him to jot down a response to one of these questions:

- The main idea of tonight's Bible study was...
- The most confusing point (muddiest point) in the passage tonight was...
- I plan to respond to tonight's Bible study by...

Purchase a supply of highlighters, preferably pink, yellow, and green...
Distribute a paper copy of the Scripture passage for the session.

Ask group members to consider the three colors of highlighters to be comparable to the three colors of a stop light: red-yellow-green. While you read the passage, highlight in pink any portion you are totally unsure of, meaning, "I need to stop and investigate this." For verses that are familiar, but you don't totally get, highlight those in yellow. If the meaning of the verse or section is familiar and you have no questions, then highlight that portion in green, meaning you are ready to Go! Circulate among your participants as they respond, making mental notes of verses/sections that are highlighted in red/pink (spend more time there...) and green (your teens feel confident in their understanding so you can pick up the pace.)[9]

The Power of *Pause:*

Following a question during the presentation of new content, don't take the fastest response or the call on the same participants all the time. Challenge your group members to assess their own level of understanding and give them adequate time to do so. In educational literature this is called "wait time." In addition to involving more respondents, this does a number of things. When the leader too quickly takes the first and fastest response, other teens stop even considering a response, predicting that the same "A" student is going to step up. In addition, a longer wait time, say 30 seconds, usually allows time for higher order thinking to take place. Lemov discusses using a "narrated wait time," in which the leader encourages and directs.[10] You can use comments like, "Look up when you think you have a response." Or "I am waiting for five more people who are ready to go." A third prod might be, "I see folks looking back at the text...that's a great idea."

》》

Nathan's takeaway:

Nathan was now committed to checking on the progress of his group on a regular basis. Their unit of study on books of the Bible that cover the history of the Post-Exilic Period was in full swing, so he decided to begin with *Whip Around*...each teen was given fifteen seconds to list the leaders of the three waves of returning exiles from Persia. Nathan instructed everyone to stand and then called on participants to give one name at a time. After the names Zerubbabel, Ezra, and Nehemiah were presented, Nathan instructed everyone having those names to sit down. After checking to see if any other names were in play, Nathan invited everyone to sit down. (Accepting "wrong answers" would give him information about possible points of confusion. Also, it would create an atmosphere where participants did not need to fear having incorrect answers.)

Next Nathan presented a ten-minute lecture on Nehemiah's prayer in chapter one of that book. Following this mini-lecture, he distributed an *exemplar* of a prayer he wrote following the pattern in chapter one. Using both prayers, his teens identified the qualities found in both and looked for any differences.

Also, using a notecard for an Exit Ticket, the teens responded to Nathan's question, "What has the Holy Spirit spoken to you tonight? What do you need to be praying for?" He collected their cards as they left and what he read brought him great joy and even a few tears. Nathan had some evidence that transformation was taking place and some great ideas about where to begin the next time the group met.

《《《

Teacher Reflection:

1. What techniques have you relied on in the past to measure the comprehension level of your group on a particular topic? Most would respond: I watch their faces and they communicate to me that they are tracking with me. Or others might add, I ask if anyone has any questions and then I clarify anything that is voiced. Can you admit that this is superficial at best and that you are taking the easy way out?

2. Pull out your last teaching outline and identify three points in the lesson in which you can insert a brief formative assessment activity the next time you use that outline.

---

[1] W. James Popham, *Transformative Assessment* (Alexandria: ASCD, 2008), 5.

[2] Judy Willis, *Research-Based Strategies to Ignite Student Learning: Insights From a Neurologist and Classroom Teacher* (Alexandria: ASCD, 2006), 82.

[3] Douglas Fisher and Nancy Frey, *Checking for Understanding: Formative Assessment Techniques for Your Classroom* (Alexandria: ASCD, 2007), 26-27.

[4] Ibid., 67.

[5] Ibid., 34.

[6] Harry Grover Tuttle, *Formative Assessment: Responding to Your Students* (Larchmont: Eye on Education, Inc. 2009), 16.

[7] Doug Lemov, *Teach Like a Champion: 49 Techniques That Put Students on the Path to College* (San Francisco: Jossey-Bass, 2010), 134.

[8] Ibid., 132.

[9] Popham, *Transformative Assessment*, 61.

[10] Lemov, *Teach Like a Champion*, 135.

Chapter 8

SO WHAT DOES THIS LOOK LIKE WHEN I PREPARE THE LESSON?

Effective teachers create a lesson plan that leads to transformation.

Things were starting to fall into place for both his prepara-tion rhythm and his teaching, but the lesson plan was not quite seamless. Nathan began his week studying the pas-sage content carefully. As he expanded his study beyond the passage itself, he picked up ideas about time and place involved in the selected verses. As the week progressed, he began considering how the material could best connect with his teens. But what he lacked was a lesson plan model that would help him snap these pieces into place. The les-son passage for his group this particular week was John's account of Jesus' encounter with the Samaritan woman in John 4. Nathan prayed that as he invested the passage he would gain fresh insights into teaching methods used by Je-sus.

Throughout this book, the thesis has been that the shared experience of teaching and learning has not taken place unless real change has occurred in the student. Closely related to this proposition is the notion that the teacher must engage his/her learner in the process of con-structing understanding. That is, lasting change is best accomplished when the pupil is actively engaged in the teaching learning process as opposed to being a passive recipient of new information. Could there be a more startling or compelling example of radical change in a person than that which took place in the life of the Samaritan woman as described in the Gospel of John?

For most contemporary readers to grasp just how extreme the transformation was that took place that day, he/she must suspend all cultural perspectives about respect between races, genders, and religious relationships. Stated succinctly, the teacher and student in the narrative were not even supposed to be in the same classroom environment together! Not to mention talking and exchanging ideas. (Bible study teachers today think they have some difficult dynamics to deal with as they prepare to teach each week!) But John 4 presents a picture of radical change in the life of a woman who had no expectation of learning anything as she mechanically carried out the most mundane of daily chores. From unsuspecting learner... to reluctant participant in a taboo conversation... to fully invested follower who became a passionate convert. Would a Bible teacher dare to dream that the Holy Spirit could possibly work through him to bring about that type of change in his students? A careful analysis of what took place during this encounter will yield a model of teaching worthy of duplication in our lesson preparation each week.

KEY #8: EFFECTIVE TEACHERS CREATE A LESSON PLAN THAT LEADS TO TRANSFORMATION.

Following the pattern of Jesus, teachers can be used by the Holy Spirit to teach in ways that transform the teenagers in their Bible study.

In this final chapter, it is time for the reader to consider assembling an entire lesson using ALTs in appropriate moments in the class period. As the author has done in each chapter, the examination and application of the teaching methods of Christ gives teachers a powerful model of effective teaching to emulate. First, we must become student teachers in Christ's classroom in order to learn from the Master Teacher. The author of this text invites you to join him on an observation visit and step into the narrative of John 4. One further point must be made—we enter the Lord's classroom, not as evaluators with the proverbial clipboard and score card, but as novice teachers hoping to learn from the Master Himself. Below are the notes this author scribbled down while watching Jesus teach.

Observation note #1: The Master Teacher (TMT) began by *connecting with the student* through a request for water. While this is odd on so many levels, the request was respectful and called for a response that the student, the Samaritan woman (SW), was capable of performing. To begin presenting information at this point would appear to be futile—the learner was not prepared to receive new material (verse 7). Engagement observed.

Observation note #2: TMT engaged his student in discussion that touched on the *context of her cultural and religious background.* The content of the exchange further highlights TMT's awareness of her mindset and schema—she has familiarity with the concept of God and the hope of Messiah (verses 9-10, 25). Active learning: class discussion.

Observation note #3: TMT also connected with *the context of the student's biblical/historical background* as revealed in the reference that she made to "our father Jacob." TMT was using the familiar to serve as a metaphor or vehicle by which He could introduce new information. He was preparing her to receive the greatest concept any teacher can share with a pupil: the identity of Christ (verses 11-12). ALT: Thinking and Problem Solving.

Observation note #4: TMT presented the *new content with a clearly defined objective*—to assist the student in reaching an awareness of His identity and making a commitment to Him. The preceding interaction as cited in Observation Notes #1-3 led seamlessly to His introduction about who He is and what a relationship with Him would mean for her life, i.e., "whoever drinks of the water that I will give him shall never thirst; but the water that I will give him will become in him a well of water springing up to eternal life" (verse 14). Further, new perspectives about worship were presented. This is a particularly difficult stage in the lesson because the new content is in direct contradiction to the student's current practice, i.e., "Woman, believe Me, an hour is coming when neither in this mountain nor in Jerusalem will you worship the Father" (verse 21). But the interaction has certainly stirred her to consider new perspectives.

Observation note #5: As new content is presented, TMT *checks the student's level of comprehension.* By giving her the opportunity to participate in dialogue, TMT allows SW to demonstrate that she is tracking with the presentation. For example, she says, "Sir, you have nothing to draw with and the well is deep" (verse 11). Then she asks Him for the living water so she will never thirst again. Yes, she has transitioned to discussing the new concept (verse 15). A further *challenge for conviction* was made—"Go, call your husband and come here" (verse 16). To which she responded correctly, "I have no husband" (verse 17). ALT: Formative Assessment.

Observation note #6: The student (SW) responded to the new insights and the transforming experience of being with Jesus in a remarkable way: she applied what she had learned as evidenced by forgetting about her original purpose for being there and heading back home to tell the men (verse 28). This dynamic *application* led to many others coming to know Jesus.

Summary of observation: The observer believes the following model best illustrates his analysis of this presentation by The Master Teacher.

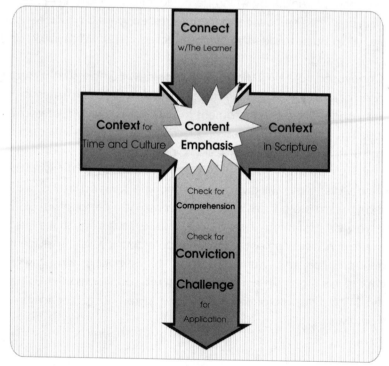

The imaginary observation concluded with the presentation of a new model: The Master's Model. Some teachers may be wondering, "Is it realistic for me to consider following a teaching outline designed around the methodologies of the Son of God?" Roy Zuck responds to this question by pointing out that though we have limitations, the fact remains we have the mind of Christ (1 Corinthians 2:16) and that the Holy Spirit is our Teacher (John 14:26; 16:12-15; 1 Corinthians 2:10-16). "We do not have perfect knowledge of the Scriptures, complete wisdom, or full insight into the human heart, but we can grow in spiritual wisdom."[1] With this admonition in mind, we take a closer look at the incredible pieces of Jesus' lesson plan. Each stage of The Master's Model will be examined beginning at the top of the cross.

Connect With the Learner:

As an effective teacher prepares the introduction of the lesson, he/she carefully considers the most meaningful way to connect with the *schema* of the learner. The reader will recall the discussion of this concept in chapter two—with what prior learning or mental structures can the teacher connect? For maximum effectiveness, the  teacher should delay planning the introduction until after researching the focal passage, the historical/cultural context, and the biblical context. From this research will flow the main concepts of the lesson; the *connection* or hook could attach to any of these areas.

In the narrative from John 4, Jesus connected with the Samaritan woman in the simplest of ways..."Give Me a drink," a request that she certainly understood, as would a person from any culture in any time period. Jesus knew there was a powerful metaphor at work in this lesson, but He was merely engaging her in conversation and interaction at the outset.

If we were introducing this passage today, we might begin with asking students to recall what they know about the relationships between the Jews and the Samaritans. A think-pair-share engagement might be effective here. (This is an example of using an Active Learning Technique (ALT) with information from the historical/cultural context as a hook at the beginning of the lesson.) Another approach would be for the teacher to engage students by asking them to list ideas about how to approach a stranger with whom you believe you have nothing in common. (Once again, using a piece of the historical/cultural context to connect with the classes' schema.)

A Tea Party (as presented in chapter three) warm up would give students the opportunity to talk to classmates and visitors about how their current style of worship compares with their previous worship experiences. In the John 4 passage, Jesus challenges the Samaritan woman to consider the past and present approaches to worship in light of the Living Water that stands before her (biblical context). Other related statements could include a focus on the misplaced energies that go into empty religious practices, a topic of discussion between Jesus and this woman.

Another Tea Party discussion could be based on the central focus of the lesson that is Jesus, the Messiah, as the One who satisfies our greatest needs and deepest longings. The discussion statements could be something like, "People I encounter at the ____ are focused on the personal need of _____. If I were able to connect with them about spiritual things, I might begin with... ." (*Content* focus for the initial *Connection*—this introduction would be designed to hook this conversation to the main objective of the lesson.)

Before moving to the second stage, the author wishes to emphasize once more the importance of *connecting with your learners*. In *Teaching Redemptively*, Donovan Graham supports this claim in a chapter entitled, "Engaging in Learning":

> Things may happen or exist apart from my awareness of them, but I cannot say I know them until I have somehow related them to myself, my experiences, and my understandings. So learning, which involves accepting something as truth to the extent that it has an impact on subsequent behavior, occurs only as learners are able to relate ideas or events to themselves."[2]

Context for Time and Culture:

Many, if not all, lessons for 21st century believers require the teacher to assist teens in dealing with unfamiliar cultural dimensions of the lessons. In the narrative under discussion Jesus' contemporaries frequently found the Savior's unconventional behavior as radical and even abhorrent. As is pointed out in the text, "Jews have no dealings with Samaritans" (John 4:9b). In the "melting pot" culture of America, such separation exists, but it is not such a familiar pattern of our way of life. The tone and meaning of her response, "How is it that You, being a Jew, ask me for a drink since I am a Samaritan woman?" (John 4:9a) could likewise be missed. R.V.G. Tasker comments on this exchange, "Her reply to Jesus' request for a drink of water has sometimes been regarded as sarcastic, as though she was saying in effect, 'So you Jews are not above asking help from us Samaritans when the need arises.' More probably it is an expression of bewilderment, 'Well here is a strange thing—a Jew asking a Samaritan for a drink'!"[3]

Context for Time and Culture

What was the basis for this animosity? Following the conquering of the Northern Kingdom of Israel around 720 B.C., the Assyrians relocated their new captives, ten of the twelve tribes of Israel. Most, but not all, of the inhabitants intermarried in the regions to which they were dispersed, and these became known as the "ten lost tribes." The small percentage that remained also intermarried with new residents of the territory and their descendants were the first century citizens of Samaria. Because of this racial impurity, they were regarded as Gentiles by the Jews who resided in Jerusalem and the Southern Kingdom.[4] This historical point could be the point of engagement. As presented in chapter three, a simple mental activity might sound like this: "Have you experienced a 'falling out' among family members that resulted in brokenness and even hostility? What behavior caused this separation? Would their children be surprised if you approached them and asked for a favor?"

Geographical information can be crucial to one's full understanding of the passage, but must be presented in small, interesting pieces, so as not to lose the attention of the class. Regarding this passage, a brief explanation of the landscape of the territory can create a richer appreciation for Jesus' appearance at this particular well. Barclay explains,

> Palestine is only 120 miles long from north to south. But within that 120 miles there were in the time of Jesus three definite divisions of territory. In the extreme north lay Galilee; in the extreme south lay Judea; and in between lay Samaria. Jesus did not wish at this stage in his ministry to be involved in a controversy about baptism; so he decided to quit Judea for the time being and transfer his operations to Galilee. The quickest way from Judea to Galilee lay through Samaria. Using that route, the journey could be done in three days. The alternative route was to cross the Jordan, go up the eastern side of the river to avoid Samaria, re-cross the Jordan north of Samaria and then enter Galilee. This was a route which took twice as long.[5]

Sketching a simple map on the board for students to look at while the teacher presents a two-minute lecture on this material would be time well spent. In addition, some students would be more engaged if given a note card and invited to copy the drawing.

Teachers are encouraged to consider the impact on comprehension that each of the concepts below might have on a student's understanding:

- Nehemiah as cupbearer to the king in Nehemiah 1:11.
- Daniel as prefect in Babylon in Daniel 2:48.
- The exalted status of the firstborn male in Genesis 27.
- Jewish traditions involved with death and burial in John 11.
- Eating meat that has been offered to idols in 1 Corinthians 8:4-13.

Context in Scripture:

An attentive student studying this narrative about the Samaritan woman would probably wonder—what is Jesus doing in Samaria? Exploring the context of the preceding verses reveal that Jesus needed to move quickly out of Judea in order to avoid

Context in
Scripture

further discussion about the growing popularity of his ministry in light of surpassing the successful, but now smaller, number of baptisms of John the Baptist. This comparison of who has the larger mega-ministry, Jesus or John the Baptist, by the Pharisees, would ratchet up the potential of the arrest of Jesus. He knew it was coming, but now was not the time. This explanation from the larger context in John clarifies what is transpiring in this passage. Another perspective is to glance back to John two and see Jesus' discussion here through the lens of the cleansing of the temple (John 2:13-25). One scholar explains, "A major feature of the cleansing of the temple finds its exposition in chapter four, namely the new order in worship brought into being through the redemptive presence and action of Christ."[6] In an even larger biblical context, in John four Jesus sets the stage for Philip and other members of the early church to witness and minister in Samaria following the stoning of Stephen in Acts eight.[7]

With this biblical context in mind, a teacher who wants to engage his teens at this juncture could invite classmates to consider a time in their lives when trouble or pressure outside of their control forced a change of plans or direction or focus. Did the events following the change produce a harvest of God-honoring results? Could they see God's hand at work in retrospect? Take thirty seconds to consider. Now turn to your "elbow partner" and take one minute to trade stories. (Review these steps in chapters three and six.) As the students speak to each other, the teacher can be watching for students who are particularly animated or expressive in communicating their answers. The teacher can call on one or more of these students during the final stage of *think-pair-share*.

Content Emphasis

Content of the Lesson:

The most significant amount of your preparation time and your instructional time needs to focus on the verses that are to be exegeted or "worked through." While the value of the interaction between classmates and teacher is important, the teacher must guard against using a disproportionate amount of time in other phases of the lesson to the detriment of a clear presentation of the truth of God's Word found in the passage designated for that study. That is the meaning behind the placement of the phrase, *content of the lesson*, at the center of the model. Reflecting on the central meaning of John 4, Gary M. Burge writes, "Converts must know how to identify the gift and its giver and converts must ask for a drink" (John 4:10). Burge continues,

> I see two dimensions to conversion here, one cognitive and one experiential. (a) The woman must be able to identify correctly who Jesus is. In theological terms, there is a doctrinal expectation. Content matters. To have a spirituality (no matter how profound) that is not based on the truth should not be trusted. "God is spirit, and his worshippers must worship Him in spirit and in truth" (4:24). (b) There is an experiential hope. To have correct theology, to be doctrinally sound and orthodox, but to have never tasted the water or to have never felt the Holy Spirit is to miss a vital component of discipleship. For John, the "head" and "heart" must be engaged.[8]

This discussion makes two major points about the lesson from John four, which are central to the thrust of The Master's Model. Burge states: "Content matters." Yes! Though we stress the concept of active engagement throughout this book, the ALTs must be focused on the truth of God's Word. Secondly, Burge states: "There is an experiential hope."[9] The theme of **transformational teaching** is that teens are more likely to construct understanding with accuracy and commitment when the teacher involves them in active learning during the class.

Insights from Mind, Brain, and Education Research

A new way to view teaching: *the art of changing the brain!*[10]

Brain-based strategies can be used to reduce the amount of rote memorization required, and what remains can be less tedious because these strategies help students access and use more effective types of memory storage and retrieval. The goal of research-based education is to structure lessons to ultimately rely less on inefficient and tedious rote memory. Helping students access and use more effective types of memory storage and retrieval will literally *change their brains*.[11] (emphasis added)

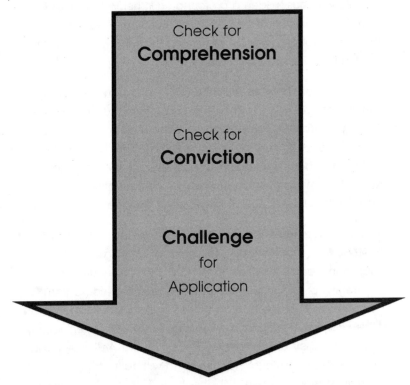

Check for
Comprehension

Check for
Conviction

Challenge
for
Application

The final pieces of your lesson plan: **Check for comprehension, Check for Conviction,** and **Challenge for Application:**

Many Bible study teachers effectively execute the first four points of *The Master's Model,* but sometimes the lesson plan ends there or time runs out before he brings out the closer. Just as Jesus was never satisfied to tell an interesting story without taking His listeners to the intersection of decision, we should plan a precise moment in which our students come face-to-face with the Truth that cuts sharper than a two-edged sword. Burge compares this aspect of John four to watching someone opening a box that contains a wound spring:

> No doubt as readers we anticipate the climax in 4:17, "I have no husband." Watching the conversation unfold is like watching someone unwrap a box in which is hidden a lively spring. When Jesus inquires about her marital status, the spring is loosed and we wonder what will happen next. Here we have a potential disciple who has hidden a profound sin in her life. Perhaps it is a way of life that must be addressed. But Jesus recognizes that there is no going forward, no reaching the living water, until this hidden thing is exposed and cleansed.[12]

All too often teachers are oblivious to the importance of confronting sin in their lives and naive to think teens can move forward and reach the living water (in the words of Burge) without confronting the sin that serves as a blockade to the rich refreshment their students desire. Or could it be that otherwise effective teachers lack the courage to push forward with a much needed moment of confrontation? Author Gary Newton challenges teachers to target heart-deep teaching:

> True learning expresses itself in life just as true belief reflects in lifestyle. It is not enough to develop learning experiences that train people to think differently, feel differently, choose differently, or act differently. Life change must come from a transformation of the heart, which includes all the dimensions of the person. Teachers must model such heart-deep learning before they can effectively teach others. Active learning experiences need to go hand in hand with reflective exercises to help students wrestle with the "whys" of various activities. Bible teaching and theological training should always be integrated cognitively, affectively, volitionally, and behaviorally. Godly thoughts, feelings, and decisions express themselves in godly behavior.[13]

In a lesson on John four, the teacher can first *check for comprehension* by asking, "Why did Jesus need to bring up the Samaritan Woman's marital relationships?" Then, the students can be challenged to consider what the Holy Spirit is prompting them to give up or change in their walk with Christ. Given the personal and potentially awkward nature of this *check for conviction*, the engagement/ALT at this point would best be done privately, in prayer, personal reflection, or a written note that remains with the writer.

Finally, a *challenge for application* brings the lesson's major idea to the point of intersection in students' lives. In the closing moments of the class session, the teacher leads students to consider what the truth of the biblical passage can become in each of their lives. A teacher might close by reading, "The woman left her water pot and went into the city and said to the men, 'Come, see a man who told me all the things that I have done; this is not the Christ, is it?' They went out of the city, and were coming to Him" (John 4:28-30). Then ask, "So we are told where she went, to whom she spoke, and what she said. Consider the *where*, the *who*, and the *what* of your presentation of the truth from this lesson this week. You have three sticky notes and a pen. Please place one of your responses to each of these questions on one of the sticky notes. When you are finished, please come up to the front of the room and place your note under the proper category—*where*, *who*, and *what*." Before the class leaves, select some of the notes and read them aloud in order to challenge and encourage the members. (Review these steps presented in chapter seven.)

It is the prayer of this author and Bible teacher that this chapter has sufficiently challenged you to continue in the pursuit of teaching like the Master. The passage from John four is compelling and inspiring: we can follow The Master's Model! Roy Zuck exhorts us to teach like Jesus in the following quote:

> Although our teaching environment, instructional situations, educational tools, and social milieu differ, much can be gained from the way he taught. How he gained interest, how he stimulated thinking, involved students, taught stories, applied truths, answered questions, dealt with individuals of varying personalities and differing attitudes toward him, motivated and corrected students—these are a few of the many areas where we can learn from his style.[14]

And learn from the Master, we must. As our students' are transformed by His Word, they will go home to their communities and compel others to come meet the Savior.

>>>

Nathan's takeaway...

Nathan had committed time each week during the previous six months for considering the **Eight Keys for Transformation** and **The Master's Model** as he prepared his Bible study. He was delighted and thankful to see transformation in the lives of his teenagers. Close to 100% were engaged each week during their Bible study, and the activities and assessments he was using revealed a deepening of their faith and an increase in their higher order thinking. He had continued to mention metacognitive strategies and occasionally heard group members describing the mental processing that was occurring as they studied. And even more remarkable was that four Bible studies at various high schools had begun recently, led by members of his group. The four teens felt that the Bible teaching presented by Nathan had prepared them to begin the journey alone. Nathan was so thankful to see members of his group being transformed to become independent, self-motivated disciples leading groups of their own.

<<<<<<<<<<<<<<<<<<<<<<<<<<<<<<<<<<<<<<<<<<<<<<<<<<<<<<<<<<<<<<<

Teacher Reflection:

1. One of the challenges behind **The Master's Model** is the need to begin early in the week to prepare your lesson outline. I call it "The Crockpot Method" of preparation—slicing new ingredients throughout the week and allowing the Holy Spirit to marinate the Word and your own experiences and observations. Make a flexible timeline for your study pattern and discuss it with a fellow teacher.

2. Nathan's takeaway above reveals that he witnessed transformation in the lives of his teenagers. Make a list of potential changes

you would like to see in your teens and ask the Holy Spirit to guide you in the assessment of their progress.

[1] Roy B. Zuck, *Teaching as Jesus Taught* (Grand Rapids: Baker Books, 1995), 14.

[2] Donovan L. Graham, *Teaching Redemptively: Bringing Grace and Truth Into Your Classroom*, 2nd ed. (Colorado Springs: Purposeful Designs Publications, 2009), 168.

[3] R. V. G. Tasker, ed., *The Gospel According to St. John: An Introduction and Commentary*, The Tyndale New Testament Commentaries (Grand Rapids: William B. Eerdmans Publishing Company, 1988), 75.

[4] William Barclay, *The Gospel of John: Volume 1*, Rev. ed., The Daily Study Bible Series (Philadelphia: The Westminster Press, 1975), 149.

[5] Ibid., 146-147.

[6] George R. Beasley-Murray, *World Biblical Commentary*, 2nd ed., Vol. 36, *John* (Nashville: Thomas Nelson Publishers, 1999), 31.

[7] Tasker, *The Gospel According to St. John*, 75.

[8] Gary M. Burge, *John: From Biblical Text... to Contemporary Life*, eds. Terry Muck et al., The NIV Application Commentary Series (Grand Rapids: Zondervan, 2000), 158.

[9] Ibid.

[10] James E. Zull, "The Art of Changing the Brain," *Educational Leadership* 62, no. 1, pg. 68 (September, 2004), http://www.ascd.org/ASCD/pdf/journals/ed_lead/el200409_zull.pdf (accessed July 27, 2016).

[11] Judy Willis, *Research-Based Strategies to Ignite Student Learning: Insights From a Neurologist and Classroom Teacher* (Alexandria: ASCD, 2006), 6.

[12] Burge, *John*, 155.

[13] Gary Newton, *Heart-Deep Teaching: Engaging Students for Transformed Lives* (Nashville: B&H Publishing Group, 2012), 192.

[14] Zuck, *Teaching As Jesus Taught*, 13.

BIBLIOGRAPHY

Ambrose, Susan A., Michael W. Bridges, Michele DiPietro, Marsha C. Lovett, and Marie K. Norman. *How Learning Works: Seven Research-Based Principles for Smart Teaching*. San Francisco: Jossey-Bass, 2010.

Anderson, Lorin W., and David R. Krathwohl et al. eds. *A Taxonomy for Learning, Teaching, and Assessing: A Revision of Bloom's Taxonomy of Educational Objectives*. Complete ed. New York: Addison Wesley Longman, Inc., 2001.

Bain, Ken. *What the Best College Teachers Do*. Cambridge: Harvard University Press, 2004.

Barclay, William. *The Gospel of John: Volume 1*. Rev. ed. The Daily Study Bible Series. Philadelphia: The Westminster Press, 1975.

Bassett, W. Philip, and Eddie K. Baumann. "Teaching Methodologies." In *Foundations of Christian School Education: Perspectives on Christian Teaching*, edited by James Braley, Jack Layman, and Ray White. Colorado Springs: Purposeful Design Publications, 2003.

Beasley-Murray, George R. *World Biblical Commentary*. 2nd ed. Vol. 36. *John*. Nashville: Thomas Nelson Publishers, 1999.

Bromiley, Geoffrey W. *Theological Dictionary of the New Testament*, Abridged In One Volume. Edited by Gerhard Kittel and Gerhard Friedrich. Grand Rapids: William B. Eerdmans Publishing Company, 1985.

Burge, Gary M. *John: From Biblical Text ... to Contemporary Life*. Edited by Terry Muck et al. The NIV Application Commentary Series. Grand Rapids: Zondervan, 2000.

Chick, Nancy. "Metacognition." Vanderbilt University Center for Teaching. http://cft.vanderbilt.edu/guides-sub-pages/metacognition/ (accessed May 20, 2014).

Coley, Kenneth S. "Active Learning Techniques in the Christian Education Classroom and in Ministry Contexts." *Christian Education Journal* 9, no. 2 (Fall 2012): 357-371.

Dean, Ceri B., Elizabeth Ross Hubbell, Howard Pitler, and B. J. Stone. *Classroom Instruction That Works: Research-Based Strategies for Increasing Student Achievement*. 2nd ed. Alexandria: ASCD, 2012.

Earl, Lorna. *Assessment as Learning: Using Classroom Assessment to Maximize Student Learning*. Thousand Oaks: Corwin Press, 2003. Quoted in Carol Ann

Tomlinson and Marcia B. Imbeau, *Leading and Managing a Differentiated Classroom*. Alexandria: ASCD, 2010.

Felder, Richard M., and Rebecca Brent. "Active Learning: An Introduction." *ASQ Higher Education Brief 2*, no. 4 (August, 2009). http://www.smith.edu/sherrerd-center/docs/ALpaper(ASQ).pdf (accessed July 21, 2016).

Fisher, Douglas, and Nancy Frey. *Checking for Understanding: Formative Assessment Techniques for Your Classroom*. Alexandria: ASCD, 2007.

Frey, Nancy, Douglas Fisher, and Sandi Everlove. *Productive Group Work: How to Engage Students, Build Teamwork, and Promote Understanding*. Alexandria: ASCD, 2009.

Graham, Donovan L. *Teaching Redemptively: Bringing Grace and Truth Into Your Classroom*. 2nd ed. Colorado Springs: Purposeful Designs Publications, 2009.

Gregory, Gayle H., and Carolyn Chapman. *Differentiated Instructional Strategies: One Size Doesn't Fit All*. 3rd ed. Thousand Oaks: Corwin, 2013.

Gregory, John Milton. *The Seven Laws of Teaching*, Rev. ed. Mansfield Centre: Martino Publishing, 2011.

Guillaume, Andrea M., Ruth Helen Yopp, and Hallie Kay Yopp. *50 Strategies for Active Teaching: Engaging K-12 Learners in the Classroom*. Merrill/Prentice Hall Teaching Strategies Series. Upper Saddle River: Pearson Merrill Prentice Hall, 2007.

Hall, Pete, and Alisa Simeral. *Teach Reflect Learn: Building Your Capacity for Success in the Classroom*. Alexandria: ASCD, 2015.

Jackson, Robyn R. *Never Work Harder Than Your Students and Other Principles of Great Teaching*. Alexandria: ASCD, 2009.

Johnson, David W., and Roger T. Johnson. *Learning Together and Alone: Cooperative, Competitive, and Individualistic Learning*. Englewood Cliffs: Prentice Hall, 1975.

Lemov, Doug. *Teach Like a Champion: 49 Techniques That Put Students on the Path to College*. San Francisco: Jossey-Bass, 2010.

MacCullough, Martha A. *By Design: Developing a Philosophy of Education Informed by a Christian Worldview*. Langhorne: Cairn University, 2013.

Mackey, Roger W. "Strategies That Promote Greater Student Engagement and Professor Enjoyment." Lecture, The Teaching Professor Annual Conference, Washington, DC, June 3, 2016.

Marzano, Robert J. *The Art and Science of Teaching: A Comprehensive Framework for Effective Instruction*. Alexandria: ASCD, 2007.

Marzano, Robert J., Debra J. Pickering, and Jane E. Pollock. *Classroom Instruction That Works: Research-Based Strategies for Increasing Student Achievement*. Alexandria: ASCD, 2001.

Mather, Emily. "Chunk-Challenge-Chew-Chat-Check." *Education Update* 57, no. 6, pg. 7 (June, 2015). http://www.ascd.org/publications/newsletters/education_update/jun15/vol57/num06/Chunk-Challenge-Chew-Chat-Check.aspx (accessed July 21, 2016).

Melick, Rick, and Shera Melick. *Teaching That Transforms: Facilitating Life Change Through Adult Bible Teaching*. Nashville: B&H Academic, 2010.

Newton, Gary. *Heart-Deep Teaching: Engaging Students for Transformed Lives*. Nashville: B&H Publishing Group, 2012.

O'Brien, Peter T. *Colossians, Philemon*. World Biblical Commentary. Edited by David A. Hubbard et al. Waco: Word Books, 1982.

Opitz, Michael F., and Michael P. Ford. *Engaging Minds in the Classroom: The Surprising Power of Joy*. Alexandria: ASCD, 2014.

Orlich, Donald C., Robert J. Harder, Richard C. Callahan, Michael S. Trevisan, and Abbie H. Brown. *Teaching Strategies: A Guide to Effective Instruction*. Boston: Wadsworth, 2010.

Popham, W. James. *Transformative Assessment*. Alexandria: ASCD, 2008.

Prince, Michael. "Does Active Learning Work? A Review of the Research." *J. Engr. Education* 93, no. 3 (July, 2004). http://www4.ncsu.edu/unity/lockers/users/f/felder/public/Papers/Prince_AL.pdf (accessed July 20, 2016). Quoted in Richard M. Felder and Rebecca Brent, "Active Learning: An Introduction." *ASQ Higher Education Brief* 2, no. 4, pg. 3 (August, 2009). http://www.smith.edu/sherrerdcenter/docs/ALpaper(ASQ).pdf (accessed July 21, 2016).

Rollins, Suzy Pepper. *Learning in the Fast Lane: Eight Ways to Put All Students on the Road to Academic Success*. Alexandria: ASCD, 2014.

Schlechty, Philip C. *Engaging Students: The Next Level of Working on the Work*. San Francisco: Jossey-Bass, 2011. Quoted in Michael F. Opitz and Michael P. Ford, *Engaging Minds in the Classroom: The Surprising Power of Joy*. Alexandria: ASCD, 2014.

Schoenback, Ruth, Greenleaf Cynthia, Murphy Lynn. *Reading for Understanding: A Guide to Improving Reading in Middle and High School Classrooms*. Jossey-Bass Education Series. Hoboken: Wiley, 1999.

Sherrin, David. *Judging for Themselves: Using Mock Trials to Bring Social Studies and English to Life*. New York: Routledge, 2016.

Sherrin, David. *The Classes They Remember: Using Role-Plays to Bring Social Studies and English to Life*. New York: Routledge, 2016.

Stronge, James H. *Qualities of Effective Teachers*. 2nd ed. Alexandria: ASCD, 2007.

Tasker, R. V. G., ed. *The Gospel According to St. John: An Introduction and Commentary*. The Tyndale New Testament Commentaries. Grand Rapids: William B. Eerdmans Publishing Company, 1988.

Tokuhama-Espinosa, Tracey. *Making Classrooms Better: 50 Practical Applications of Mind, Brain, and Education Science*. New York: W. W. Norton & Company, Inc., 2014.

Tomlinson, Carol. *How to Differentiate Instruction in Mixed-Ability Classrooms*. Alexandria: ASCD, 2001.

Tuttle, Harry Grover. *Formative Assessment: Responding to Your Students*. Larchmont: Eye On Education, Inc., 2009.

Willis, Judy. *Research-Based Strategies to Ignite Student Learning: Insights From a Neurologist and Classroom Teacher*. Alexandria: ASCD, 2006.

Wilson, Donna, and Marcus Conyers. *Five Big Ideas for Effective Teaching: Connecting Mind, Brain, and Education Research to Classroom Practice*. New York: Teachers College Press, 2013.

Wright, N. T. *The Epistles to the Colossians and to Philemon: An Introduction and Commentary*. Tyndale New Testament Commentaries. Edited by Canon Leon Morris. Grand Rapids: William B. Eerdmans Publishing Company, 1986.

Yount, William R. *Created to Learn: A Christian Teacher's Introduction to Educational Psychology*. 2nd ed. Nashville: B&H Academic, 2010.

Zuck, Roy B. *Teaching as Jesus Taught*. Grand Rapids: Baker Books, 1995.

Zull, James E. "The Art of Changing the Brain." Educational Leadership 62, no. 1 (September, 2004). http://www.ascd.org/ASCD/pdf/journals/ed_lead/el200409_zull.pdf (accessed July 27, 2016).